MW01251135

Crisis: Identity

Delta McNeish

Do you want to feel good every day?

Then *STOP* the **Crisis,**

Get your **"Identification card"** and come back home!

Welcome home stranger!

Crisis: Identity

By: Delta McNeish M/CE

An invitation to come home!

Copyright © 2008 by Delta McNeish M/CE

Crisis: Identity
by Delta McNeish M/CE

Printed in the United States of America

ISBN 978-1-60647-094-7

All rights reserved solely by the author. The author guarantees all contents are original and do not infringe upon the legal rights of any other person or work. No part of this book may be reproduced in any form without the permission of the author. The views expressed in this book are not necessarily those of the publisher.

Bible Quotations are King James Version taken from *Dakes Annotated Bible*. Copyright © 1963 by Finis Jennings Dake.

Contact delta@intercessionministries.org for more information.

Book web site: www.crisisidentity.net

Intercession Ministries web site:
www.intercessionministries.org

Heart 2 Heart Counselling Services web site:
www.heart2.org

www.xulonpress.com

Table of contents

Identity

I opened my eyes and I could now see
A great big world that meant nothing to me.
I ate, I laughed, I cried and I played.
They checked to see how much I weighed.
They picked me up they put me down.
They laughed with every baby sound.
On my own turf, I began to walk.
Crying for attention failed, so I began to talk.
I got what I wanted by being mischievous.
And learnt a lot from my parents' behaviours.
The "sandbox school" was quite a place.
With all my peers I began the race.
Laying down the standard of "all for me"
Worked very well 'til after three.
It seemed to fit well in a world of greed.
To the voice inside I gave no heed.
Deep inside was a cry for better things.
My own? Not sure! Perhaps those my mother brings.
I want to end this poem, but I'm not sure how.
For questions still linger in my head now.
The path that I am on, did I really choose it?
Did it, from birth, come from those I lived with?
Or did their reality become my identity.
I will keep digging to find the nitty-gritty.

Introduction

The purpose of writing this book is to explain why, despite our technological advances, our scientific progress, our high-tech educational systems that we call "the best in the world," we can't get along with one another. This is a huge problem! Come with me on a ride of your life and receive information and strategies that will help to validate and identify your life. Conflicts are everywhere; in churches, schools, places of business, parliament, factories, institutions, farms, homes, offices, —everywhere. It is a known fact that we have not learned how to get along with one another. Why? Why? Why?

We have enough material on human behaviours. Millions of books have been written on why and how we should behave in order to respect one another. Yet I continue to hear of strife and killing all over the world. Even law-makers are not able to pull together so we can realize world peace. That tells me that these problems can only be solved by returning to the drawing board of the Almighty God and begin to follow the plans that He has had in place since the beginning of time. It is quite obvious that man-made religions have the potential to cause more conflict than they can solve. It is also a known fact that many churches have failed to do as Jesus said (i.e. love as He loves). It might not be too late for us to start repairing the damages that have been done. While the world scrambles to halt and repair environmental damages, it seems smart to me to begin this feat inside ourselves.

My hope is that, after you read this material, you will look into your heart and begin to understand that you have been made a wonderful person who needs to ___identify___ and validate yourself in the same way that God does. This will bring a feeling of being at ___home.___ When this happens, all conflict ceases in you, and because it ceases in you, it ceases around you. This does not mean that conflict will be totally avoidable in every area of your life. It simply means that you will have the tools to deal in a Godly and professional manner with the conflicts that come and that you will not become a crisis... I am shocked at the efforts made by so many people to establish world peace when, in their own relationships, war prevails. I believe that in order to have world peace we must have peace in our hearts and in our homes. Jesus said in the Gospel of St. John 14:27 *"Peace I leave with you, my peace I give unto you: not as the world giveth, give I unto you."* In *Him* we find peace and discover our true ___Identity___. As long as there is a ___crisis: identity___ in the lives of individuals, they are not at ___home,___ and because they are not at ___home___ they will allow all kinds of abuses and violations into their lives. At ___home___ means having a Godly sense of personhood. Knowing that you are made in God's image and knowing who God has made you to be will result in God- honouring behaviour. This is your "Identification Card."

As mentioned before we already have the instructions on how to get along with one another, so you may ask yourself, why do you need this book? Good question!! The answer is in the book—just read on. Many of the methods shown here have helped me in my personal struggle to reach a place where I know myself, and I like myself. This was not the case when I was a child, a young adult, even up to the age of fifty five. Looking back in retrospect, I wish there was a book that would have helped me to get rid of all, or some, of my child-hood pain. This pain prevented me from enjoying many years of my life and caused a lot of negative behaviours. I lived with pain hidden deep inside me which was there for a long time and I did not know how to get rid of it. At that time I would look in the mirror and literally despise myself because so many awful things had traumatized me into a self-loathing conundrum... It may be difficult for those who have not experienced childhood trauma to understand the dynamics of "trauma related self- hatred." ***It is real!*** This experience is called ***Traumatic Pain Cycle***. Trauma ➔ Self-separation ➔ Pain-burial ➔ Self-hate ➔ Negative behaviours ➔ more pain ⬅. Childhood trauma can separate a person from their real self. This state of abandonment causes a fictional self or *phantom self* to develop. Many people that have been abused live in that state of separation and abandonment until they regain their true identity in God. If this identity is not regained, they will continue to live in a state of shame, guilt and blame, detached from self and totally unprepared for real life.

Ideally, if someone is going on a safari they would carefully plan the trip by detailing all the things that they need to make the trip successful. Life is a safari of sorts and it behoves all of us to strategically and methodically plan to have successful lives and not just to survive. We know that life is full of unplanned situations and surprises that happen every day, but life without a plan is, in itself, a plan to fail. As adults, we have the awesome responsibility to find the tools that will help us to become who we are meant to be. Parents and care-givers have a tremendous responsibility to lay the proper foundation that will start their children on the *safari* of life and provide them with the proper tools so they can succeed and not fail. Adults that have experienced child-hood difficulties can use the tools offered here to launch their lives like a rocket into effectiveness and celebration. As we know, success is not measured by material wealth. It is measured by our Godly behaviour. Surprise!! Our behaviour tells us about the way we think and the way that we think confirms our belief systems. Our belief systems are our foundational principles or our road-map. I am pleased to present information that contains the possibility of making life a total celebration of success, if you choose to use it. Enjoy the trip!

Chapter 1

Where Was God When I Was Hurting?

Where was God when I was hurting? I have asked this question many times in the past when my life was in chaos; both as a child and as an adult. Where was He when I was being abused? When people ask me these questions, I understand that they, like myself, are facing mega doses of disappointment; the kind of disappointment that boils up inside like a volcano spitting out large doses of let down and confusion. I lived with the sense of being disappointed for a long time. Disappointment is the root cause of most feelings of depression. Something happened that should not have happened and something should have happened that didn't. It is important to mention here that God cannot disappoint us; neither does He push his way into our lives. He must be invited in. You may ask how a child can protect herself from her abusers. She cannot. That is why God provided parents and care-givers. You may also say that, as an adult, I prayed, I believed, and yet nothing happened. I still had to face difficult situations. I believe that whenever we call upon God He is there to help us. It has been very liberating for me to understand that all of God's dealings with us are strategic. Therefore our lives have to line up with His plans. In other words, when God is involved in our lives the first thing that He will do is to give us clear directions to follow. Most people will do what they want, when they want and then involve God in what they want to do when they want to do it. This doesn't work!

God is with us when we hurt but He has chosen to put himself in a perimeter where He has to be invited in and His will must be the primary focus of our hearts. Then, by His Holy Spirit and only by His leading, things fall into place. Holy Spirit was not sent here to fix the things that we have messed up. He was sent to groom, guard and guide us, but never to govern us. The truth is some of the bad things that are happening in the world and in our lives are misinterpreted as God's mistakes. Many tend to blame God and accuse Him of things of which He is not guilty. If a person is in the will of God when a difficult situation takes place, there is no doubt that God is with them in that situation. Because they are in His will, God is wherever His will is done. This is the truth. There is no reason for God to renege on His promise of being with His children all the time. What He says He does. It is up to us to put ourselves in, or out of His will. In His will we experience His peace. There are times when God will allow His children to go through difficulties, but not without His purpose, provision, presence, power and peace.

I have found it to be so comforting to have the heavenly team, God the Father, God the Son and God the Holy Spirit, on my side. This is my place of safety. Many years ago I was not able to make this a personal confession. I was trapped in a grimy prison of fear, shame, confusion and unbelief (to name a few). I was unable to crawl my way out and to believe that God cared about me.

I was a much abused child, beaten severely by my mother to the drawing of blood; sexually abused by a hired hand of my grandmother and raped at the age of sixteen in my own home by a family friend. Left scarred, lonely and ashamed, I became very angry at God especially when there was no one to talk to. One thing sexual abusers will do is to deliberately put a blanket of silence over the one they abuse by demanding that the abused tell no one or they will get in trouble. This will always result in an inner paralysis. I was left feeling that it was my fault and this complicated matters for me because the guilt and shame was tremendous. These negative emotions resulted in more disappointment, anger and self-hatred. This cycle is also called the ***Rabbit- hole***. In order to release some of the pain I cried a lot and contemplated suicide often. In those days one did not reveal the "family's dirty laundry" so I became demoralized and I felt like a non-person. Many times I would look in the mirror and literally ask myself, who are you? My God-given identity and image was lost; my sense of person-hood shattered, my ability to love myself was gone and I became a *reactor,* angry, empty and without any personal identity. I left ***home!*** ***Home*** represents the inner person. I left myself because it was too uncomfortable to stay so I lived in a fictional self for many years.

I recall my mother telling me, whenever I was misbehaving as a child, that, if I refused to obey, she would send me to a far country where a lot of bears lived and they would eat me. She also said that I would never see her or the rest of my family again. This terrified me so much that I had nail-biting nightmares for a long time. I literally encountered these black bears in my dreams as they would chase me, causing me to wake up sweating and gasping for breath. There were many nights of horror as I tried frantically to escape. This state of mental torture made havoc of my mind and my life as I began to equate the nightmares to situations in real life. For a while I was not able to tell the difference between dream experiences and real life experiences. They were so much alike. Living felt like one big torture chamber full of "out of my control" situations. I was not able to rationalize how a loving God could stand by and watch as one little girl would hurt so much. To add more pain and confusion, I often heard the adults around me saying, in response to every negative behaviour, "God is watching everything that you do." This begged the question, "If He really sees what I am doing, then why does He refuse to help me?"

Many nights I would soak my pillow with tears before going to sleep. Question after question flooded my mind. I tried to come up with some good reasons for my presence on the earth. There must be something to life beside abuses. There were many!

When we go through difficulties it causes us to feel as though we are the only one suffering; and we begin to think that life is very unfair. I am not a judge on the fairness or unfairness of life, but this I do know now; God does not use human standards of judgment for our life situations. *His ways are much higher than ours,* but for me life was just one big puzzle. We tend to use standards of fairness and unfairness, good and bad, right and wrong, appropriate and inappropriate, kind and unkind or many others to evaluate life's situations. Anyone who can hold the stars in their places and keep this universe in perfect order and balance cannot be using human abilities, standards, judgments and intelligence. If He is, we are in trouble!

At sixteen, while still in school trying to get my education, two men proposed to me within two days, one on Sunday, and the other on Tuesday. They had already spoken to my parents, as the custom was that the parents were asked for the woman's hand in marriage first, and then the woman is asked. I did not feel that I was ready for marriage but my parents told me to marry the first man that had asked. I was so confused. The truth is I felt like they took the diapers off me at (sixteen years old) and then put me in bed with a strange man that I only knew for three months. We never dated. We never went out anywhere together, not even once. I felt so abandoned by my parents. This crippling feeling was my companion for a long time. Abandonment is an awful feeling. It is one of the root emotions that cause people to get into abusive relationships and stay there. My parents had eight children (one died at one month old). We were poor and I felt desperate and wondered why I had to be married so early in life.

Facing the world at sixteen as a married woman with no support was a devastating experience. The religious community in England, of which I was a part at that time, was very regimental, legalistic and critical. As a young person growing up in the church, I saw the adults as something from another planet. They were unapproachable, stern and very religious. They would jump and shout on Sunday morning but, during the week, their behaviour left a lot to be desired. Fights in the homes and gossip were common place. It all felt uncomfortable to me. It is nothing short of a miracle that I survived.

As a child in Jamaica, I recall doing so many things to gain the approval of my parents; one in particular still stands out in my mind. When my father returned from work in the evenings I would wash his feet. This was my plea to hear him say something nice to me. I never heard the words, "I love you," from my parents. My father was a quiet man, very gentle in spirit. In my opinion my mother was a perfectionist. Everything had to be a certain way. She was also one who did not "wait until father got home" to deal with those who broke the rules of the house. I broke several of them and paid severely. Looking back in retrospect, I believe that most of my negative behaviour as a child was a cry for parental approval. This I never received. The shrubs around our house in Jamaica were missing many branches, but not from storms or a hurricane. They were the "rods of correction" that were used to inflict pain by my mother.

Food was far more scarce than beatings and hunger was present a majority of the time. It seems that I was always on the look-out for a snack, a treat, or even the odd egg from the bony legged chickens that my grandmother raised. I recall hearing them sing "Craw, Craw, Craw, Craw," after laying an egg. My scrawny sisters and I would run for all that we were worth to the area where the noise was coming from in order to see who would be the first to find the egg. Life was very harsh in Jamaica, but life took on a different meaning of ___*harshness*___ when most of my family immigrated to England in the sixties. A new school, racism and a pre-planned marriage for a sixteen year old was all very frightening.

Three years later I would make another move. This time it was to a place that I thought was the coldest place on God's earth, Canada. This did not improve my desperate personal life dilemmas but, to the contrary, it increased my isolation and loneliness. I found that, in Canada, one can live next door to someone for years and not as much as know her name.

I was able to run for my life from the abusive marriage, but life in Montreal in 1963 was unbearable, cruel and Jamaica-like. There was no place to live, no money, no family and no friends. It was horrible. Deserted by the husband I married at sixteen, I scrambled like a hobo to find shelter. Pregnant with our third child, I found myself knocking on the doors of the *system* for housing and financial help.

When the domestic violence in the marriage was at its peak, I was told that wife abuse and domestic violence was just that, "*domestic,*" and there was nothing the law could do about it. Things were very challenging for women in abusive relationships in the sixties. One night, about 10 pm, I was struck by my husband and I ran to my neighbour's house for temporary shelter. I was so glad when she welcomed me in. She worked the eleven to seven shift and, when she left for work, I thought her husband and children were tucked away in their beds, but, as soon as she was out the door, I found myself physically fighting off her husband who tried to rape me. Although my screams frightened him away I felt that I had gone from the frying pan into the fire.

I still recall the brutal experiences of being penny-less. Not possessing the twenty cents required to take a bus from down-town Montreal to Lachine, I had to walk. When my monthly welfare check of sixty five dollars got lost in the mail, I had to walk to the office in Lachine to report it. When I finally arrived there they told me that they did not believe the check was lost. They thought that I was lying in order to get more money. Forty five dollars of that check was to cover the rent that I was supposed to pay for a roach infested bachelor apartment that I would lose if the rent was not paid. Never did it cost me so much to live with those unwelcomed roach-guests who came out to party in the night and eat my food, leaving my already shattered nerves in fragments. I had a huge fear of bugs. I was too scared to fall asleep at night, fearing that the roaches (who seemed to own the building) would evict me. I watched in horror, crouched in one corner of the room, as they feasted and changed shifts, leaving me wondering if they were the "bears" that my mother said would "get me" for not behaving well when I was a child.

Day-time brought to me a sigh of relief as the roaches temporarily slid into their roach-holes waiting for night time to arrive and party again. I will never forget my first night in that apartment. I had struggled for a long time to find a place to live. In those days, land-lords would advertise a place for rent and when you called they would say the place was available; but sadly, as soon as they saw a black face, it had suddenly been rented. After a long search, I found this small bachelor apartment. The land-lord told me that it had recently been painted. It didn't look too bad even though it was in a slummy area of town. I thought it was still better than staying on the street where I had been living. I bought a few groceries with my welfare check and put them in the cupboard, feeling very proud that I am now in an apartment. WOW!

Night brought the familiar fear of the dark but I turned off the lights anyway and blackness shrouded the room. (I had no money for a night-light.) I was about to release myself in the arms of the proverbial sandman when I heard small noises. My biggest fear was that it could be a mouse. Terrified, I got up and nervously turned on the light as my pulse rate shot up to a point where it too was a concern. Reluctantly, I went in the direction of the noise, only to find that both the inside and outside of the cupboard was covered with what appeared to be thousands of generations of roaches. My heart still pounding, I retreated back in a corner of the bed, pulled the covers over my head and wondered what I was going to do. I thought, ok guys, you can have anything that you want, just don't come over here. That was my first of many sleepless nights in that place. After I reported the problem, the land-lord refused to do anything about my unwelcome guests. Finances and joblessness was at a critical point and it also seemed that the roaches decided to live without paying rent while I could not, so when the money ran out I had to go to a shelter. This was all happening while I was pregnant.

When my daughter was born, the Doctor told me that, because I did not have a place to stay, they were not going to allow me to take her out of the hospital. It felt like a dagger went through my stomach. "Where is God now?" I cried. The pain was horrific. I suppose He was in the same place where He was when His own Son cried *"my God, my God, why hast thou forsaken me?"* Reluctantly, I went to the Salvation Army to live and did the work of a *char woman*, earning about ten dollars a day. In the evenings I would travel thirty kilometres on the train from down-town Montreal to Lachine to visit my child who was in the care of foster parents. Unprepared for the challenging Montreal weather, with inadequate winter gear and no proper boots, I arrived frozen. The pain leaking from my heart caused tears on my cheeks that were also frozen.

In 1966, while living in another run-down rooming-house in Montreal, the Lord came to me and my life was totally transformed. He revealed Himself to me in such a phenomenal manner that there was no way I could ever deny His reality. I needed this encounter because my life was hanging in the balance. It was at this point that I began to realize that God was interested in me as a person. Times of fellowship in prayer were so powerful and exciting. My life, on a spiritual level, went to a totally higher dimension and I began to realize my purpose in life. God became so real to me even though life was still difficult.

As already stated, it was very hard for a black person to find accommodation in Canada, so I remained in a rooming house for a while. I felt like a failure; lost and forgotten. Holy Spirit was the One who made my life worth living. He became very real to me. His presence in my life was the catalyst that took my life back from destruction to being identifiable. Many times my heart was numb and cold. Only His wonderful presence made the difference in my life and made life worth living.

Let us talk for a moment about the comfort that Holy Spirit brings. This is where the rubber meets the road. Jesus said that He would send another Comforter in the person of Holy Spirit after He left.

> *"If you love me, keep my commandments. And I will pray the Father and He shall give you another Comforter, that He may abide with you forever; Even the Spirit of truth whom the world cannot receive, because it seeth Him not, neither knoweth Him; but you know Him; for He dwelleth with you, and shall be in you."[1]*

When someone special is leaving, people usually cling to his[41] very last words because of their desire to carry out that individual's wishes. These are some of Jesus' parting words. Should we not be paying more attention to them? The fact is that Jesus said Holy Spirit would play a significant part in our connection with Him, so I hooked into this reality and decided to get to know Holy Spirit. The journey has been exciting.

Holy Spirit, being the perfect gentleman, will not push His way into human lives, but waits for us to allow Him to do that which is necessary. This takes place on the individual as well as the collective levels. He also draws us closer to the Father; to a place that we are not able to go by ourselves, making the Father very real to us. On the individual level, through constant fellowship with Him, a bonding takes place. I am referring here to the kind of fellowship that moves one from performing for God to *being with God*. This is the message that Jesus gave His life for. It is the message that the people of His time on the earth were not able to receive. This is the same message that many are still refusing to believe today. This is not religion. It is fellowship with God. This was explained by the Apostle Paul. We are all God's children not by creation only, but by living in constant communion with Him through His Spirit. *He writes:*

> *"But when the fullness of time was come, God sent His Son, made of a woman, made under the law, to redeem them that were under the law, that we might receive the adoption of sons. And because we are sons, God hath sent forth the Spirit of His Son into our hearts, crying Abba, Father."*[2]

It is this experience with God as "Father" that ends the personal struggle to "hit the ball" and confirms that life is one big *home run* from start to finish, even when life seems to be going out of control. Many people, like me, grew up with the idea that, unless they performed a certain way, they will not have the approval of their parents. For Jack Frost it was true. He writes:

> *"Dad was a respected man in our community, and his athletic abilities—particularly his skills as a professional tennis instructor—won him plenty of honours in Daytona Beach. I tried to reach my dad's expectations in sports and to perform well enough to earn his approval, but I was awkward with the tennis racquet and never seemed to impress him. Dad regularly reminded me—in harsh words—that I wasn't good enough.*
>
> *He would scream at me like a drill sergeant when we practiced on Saturday mornings: Put your arm into it! Be a monster! Don't be such a wimp!"*
>
> *These ordeals would leave me in tears. I felt like such a failure, yet I wanted Dad's approval so much I kept striving to perform for him. If only I could hit the ball right, I told myself, then Dad would be proud of me. I did not realize that an ungodly belief (stronghold) was growing stronger and stronger in me. I was slowly being consumed by a deep fear of failure and rejection, a fear that caused me to feel worthless unless I performed well enough to win my father's approval."[3]*

This consciousness established in childhood is sometimes carried into our adult lives and causes many who are seeking approval to carry out many tasks that God did not request them to do, when all along, they are approved by Him. It also causes some to become competitive in the ministry. This leads to the "vulture consciousness" resulting in controlling and demanding behaviours. Others possess the "I can do it all" mentality and of course we must not forget the "thunder watcher." *Jack Frost explains:*

> *"My commitment to "the ministry" was far greater than my commitment to my wife, my children or any other loving relationships. When I was at home, I was irritable and impossible to get along with. Everything I did was tainted with a passive anger.*
>
> *My countenance became stern and serious, and my preaching became legalistic and demanding. I focused on biblical truth, but my heart was empty of love. I knew the theology of God's love, but I had not experienced it in my relationships. I could quote verses in Scripture about His unconditional acceptance of us, but it was a foreign concept to me."[4]*

Having parental approval sets the stage for us to accept the approval that is already in place from God. God's approval is like a "blue-print or a road-map to follow. If I was made aware of this as a child, I probably would not have wondered where God was when I was going through so much pain. Things may have been a little clearer.

You may be wondering by now, if God can come so close to someone, why did He not help me to escape the child-hood dilemmas and those later in life? The child-hood experience I can't explain totally, but later on in life He became my best friend. Can anyone have a better friend than God? No! God is the best friend anyone could ever have. He is the only one that we can count on at all times. He keeps His word, never fails and is always dependable. It is an oxy-moron to attribute such negative thinking, as blame for not being there when we are hurting, toward God.

For some people it is easier to blame God than to take the time to find out the source of their problems or even to seek God to have a relationship with Him. When we do we will find that God is wherever His will is, to help those who are willing to work with Him. His will, being His Word, is dependable.

God's will is not being done in all things; for example, it is not the will of God for people to hurt each other but it goes on every day all over the world. Trillions of dollars have been spent in the process of hurting people through wars and killing. God is everywhere and He sees everything even though His will is not being done. We know that He has a reason and purpose for all things and, as mentioned before, He will not arbitrarily interfere in human affairs...

Many blame God for the catastrophes in the world such as famines. How can we? We only have to look at our level of greed, selfishness and waste, to realize that we all have a will, which God will not violate. Is it not in our hands to make a difference in the world? I am not blaming anyone, because I know that many have worked vigorously to quell the on-going tide of war, famine and starvation in the world; and sometimes we wonder if these issues will ever end. God's will is His Word and He gave His Son to die so that we can have abundant life. He gave His Holy Spirit that we can enjoy eternal life beginning right here on the earth. If we desire to do His will and to see things change for better, then we must get to know Holy Spirit and He will connect us to God's will. With His help we can realize greater and more positive changes in the world.

My childhood abuses have helped me to be more caring, kind and understanding of human suffering. By this I know that good can come from what may appear to be evil. I do believe that parents need to be very vigilant over their children in order to protect them from harm.

No wealthy people

The world continues to struggle with problems of starvation and many other things,
Yet I continue to here that millions of dollars are won and earned by several people all the time.
Many people say that the world is full of wealthy people.
To this I strongly disagree.
I know that most people won't agree with my philosophy,
But in my opinion, there is not one wealthy person on the earth; we are all paupers,
Because, until every human being on this earth has his basic needs met, there are no wealthy people here on the earth.
That is, if you see wealth as good behaviour that is pleasing to God, being connected and sharing all we have with Him and His creation in "oneness."

Delta McNeish 2007

The experiences of our child-hood whether positive or negative form the foundation of our lives. Mine was brutal. I have since learned that we can choose to stay in the negative mind-set or move on with God's help towards being more positive. I did. It took a long time, lots of effort, strategies, plans and prayers. The strategies given here have helped to move my life forward and, I give all the glory to God for His love and care and for the help of Holy Spirit who brought me out of the "prison" that I was in. I have forgiven my mother, because she too may have had a lot of pain.

As a Counsellor, I have seen and heard many things, none of which I will detail here, but I do have one observation that must be documented for the sake of clarity when working through difficulties. A strategy is only worthwhile when it has been applied. These strategies have helped many clients. Some people will ask for help and will tell you that they will do that which has been discussed and agreed upon. When they return for more help, it is discovered that the plan was not followed or even looked at. If the strategies presented here are applied they will work.

<u>This model will help to keep "Personal cohesiveness" in place.</u>

Model # 1

1. Make every effort to understand that God is never at fault when we run into trouble. He is impeccable, and faultless.

2. Know your purpose in life; things that you are passionate about, and find ways do them.

3. Get rid of the self-blame and shame mentality. Blame and shame are like an *M16* Gun; they will shoot you down and keep you down. Take responsibility for your mistakes, (not the mistakes of others) deal with them, make closure with them and move on.

4. When you make closure with a problem (i.e. put it behind you) remember to deliberately replace the negative emotions with positive ones. The old will return looking for its former home, so fill the previously damaged space in your heart with new desires, choices and determinations. This is very important for, if it is not done, the old, negative emotions will return.

5. Allow yourself time to work through the problems, especially those that are within your ability to control.

6. Do not allow anyone to hold you captive for things done in the past. God doesn't. He forgave you a long time ago.

7. Make informed acceptance of issues that come to your life. In other words don't accept every situation. Know why you are accepting the ones you do and be totally informed.

8. Know that everything God does is strategic and purposeful. He does not make mistakes.

Chapter 2

Feeling Safe

❖❖❖

I will begin this chapter with the much loved <u>Psalms 23:1-6</u>

"The LORD is my shepherd; I shall not want.
He maketh me to lie down in green pastures:
he leadeth me beside the still waters.
He restoreth my soul: he leadeth me in the paths of
righteousness for his name's sake.
Yea, though I walk through the valley of the
shadow of death, I will fear no evil: for thou art
with me; thy rod and thy staff they comfort me.
Thou preparest a table before me in the presence of
mine enemies: thou anointest my head with oil;
my cup runneth over.
Surely goodness and mercy shall follow me all the
days of my life: and I will dwell in the house of
the LORD for ever."[5]

Presented here are some of the most comforting words ever penned. Looking at David's plight when Saul's plan was to kill him, these words must have been so comforting to him. Knowing that his God was there and that he could trust Him in times of crisis must have been very reassuring for him. These words are still as riveting, powerful, heart-warming and meaningful as ever; however, there are times when, even though we know and understand the truth of these words, an unusual situation will cause us to forget. We get hit hard and it "rocks our boat" (so to speak). The words of the Scripture are there but they go right out the window. Those are the times when it seems that we will not make it to the next day because things appear to be so dark. We need to be prepared for such times because they come to all of us at some point in life. Having a sense of safety during these times is not just a bonus; it is paramount to moving forward.

We also need the assurance that God's track record is impeccable. He never fails. Looking at the experiences of others, such as the Prophet David who trusted and experienced God's presence will also help us. We also need friends and family that are dependable. How, then, can we come to trust the Lord and have a sense of safety? I believe it takes time and help from Holy Spirit. Time also is needed to know who we are and how we can deal with our life's issues. Have we learned how to work with Holy Spirit to let His comfort lead us to safety? He is a perfect gentleman and waits for our invitation to come into our lives. Do we give ourselves words that will cause our hearts to feel good? Words such as, "What can I learn from this?" or "The Lord who is my shepherd is with me" Or do we practice ***shoulda-therapy***. This is where we tend to blame ourselves and live in an atmosphere of regret. "I ***shoulda*** done this, I ***shoulda*** done that." Our hearts take seriously every defining moment that comes, so, when a difficult situation comes our way that is when we need the most support. Defining moments are times when a crisis brings negative feelings to the fore-front of our minds, leaving us with a sense of shock and regret; a sense that we failed. It seems that we start to beat up on ourselves in these critical times. It is no wonder that we feel sad and depressed so much of the time. ***Shoulda-therapy*** works very well? It will cast a shadow of despair over our lives that will need the positive therapy to counter it and remove the damage done by it.

If we look at folks that have had a long life embedded in self- incrimination, we are looking at people with chronic ***shoulderism.*** They need people with gentle spirits and loving hearts to help heal their wounds: people with experience in helping the wounded. There is a story in the Bible of some men who brought a sick friend to Jesus. When they could not get to Him because of the crowd, they smashed the roof and let him down on his bed in front of Jesus. This is called ***roof top therapy***. ***Roof top therapy*** is given by people who understand people and care for people from the heart.

> *"And when they could not come nigh unto him for the press, they uncovered the roof where he was: and when they had broken it up, they let down the bed wherein the sick of the palsy lay. When Jesus saw their faith, he said unto the sick of the palsy, Son, thy sins be forgiven thee."[6]*

This message of giving care is so needed. We see a lot of people who are in pain no matter where we go, but they have few people that are safe enough to talk to. When someone with a problem finds enough courage to come to us for help he needs to feel safe. He deserves to have spiritually and professionally trained individuals to help him. Trained people are needed to go into ***roof top therapy*** mode and are willing to go the whole way until those that they are helping feel better.

In David's case he acknowledged the Lord in the midst of his crisis. Confessing *that God was his shepherd* tells us that David had also learned to encourage himself in the Lord. He did this, not only when Saul was chasing him, but also when his own people were against him.

> *"And David was greatly distressed; for the people spake of stoning him, because the soul of all the people was grieved, every man for his sons and for his daughters: but David encouraged himself in the Lord."[7]*

In a world of deception and mistrust, we will have to depend on the direction of Holy Spirit to bring us to "safe people," people who have been trained to be caring and know the needs of those who come for help. They will not put us at risk for more pain by trying to do what they are not trained to do, and they will not use us for referees while they compete for thunder. Thunder stealing is a big problem in today's society. Many are looking for instant gratification by receiving the applause of the crowd. They put the lives of those in need at risk because they are not qualified to deal with their issues but they will not refer them to more appropriately trained professionals because they want to be honoured as the healer.

Jesus said that He would send "another Comforter" who would stay with us forever. This person would be instrumental in impacting our lives toward safety and closeness to God.

"Nevertheless I tell you the truth; it is expedient for you that I go away: for if I go not away, the Comforter will not come unto you; but if I depart, I will send him unto you....Howbeit when he, the Spirit of truth, is come, he will guide you into all truth, for he shall not speak of himself: but whatsoever he shall hear, that shall he speak: and he will show you things to come."[8]

Familiarizing ourselves with Holy Spirit, the third person of the God-head would be the key to being with safe people and ensuring personal safety. Having this God-ordained person in our lives guiding us constantly would eliminate the stress of knowing who to trust. We have the privilege and advantage of being guided by Holy Spirit. This wonderful Spirit of God is the best friend any one could have. I have proven Him to be very real and comforting throughout my years.

The church is supposed to be the safest place for one to bring their needs and find solace and comfort, but of late it has become a very frightening place to many. This can change if we are willing to learn how to stop beating up one another and how to give support and affirmation instead. Dr. John Townsend and Dr. Henry Cloud write:

"Fighting the good fight" is discouraging, and we often need direct encouragement from God and His Word [(Romans 15:4; Phil. 2:1).] But the Bible also emphatically says that we need to be encouraged by each other. "Tychicus, the dear brother and faithful servant in the Lord, will tell you everything, so that you also may know how I am and what I am doing. I

am sending him to you for this very purpose, that you may know how we are, and that we may encourage you." (Eph. 6:21-22)9

Some may think that this is idealistic because this is not happening now as it should. The fact is that we desperately need to encourage each other all the time. This is vital to our foundation, stability and safety; both personally and collectively. On the other side of the coin (so to speak) it becomes a conundrum for those in need of safe people when they come in contact with negativity, criticism, gossip and control instead.

We need one another in order to grow on all levels of human functions, and we do grow when we are in healthy relationships and feel safe. Relationships that are safe are the *nursery* for healthy human growth. Outside of relationships we grow wild and become unmanageable. In relationships we develop trust and character. Relationships can be seen as the *wheat and tares* of growing together because difficulties come to help us grow. The story of the *wheat and the tares in the Bible* is powerful. Jesus used this analogy to show us that when the behaviour of another person bothers us it is not necessarily the other person that we should deal with. It is our selves. This reminds me of something that I heard some time ago. *"I see something in you that I don't like about myself."* This means that, when other people's behaviours bother us, two things are happening. One: They are tapping into our ***pain control basin***, and two: They are in control of our emotions. They have the power to make us react. *Jesus spoke to this in Matthew 13: 24-30*

"Another parable put he forth unto them, saying, The kingdom of heaven is likened unto a man which sowed good seed in his field: But while men slept, his enemy came and sowed tares among the wheat, and went his way.

But when the blade was sprung up, and brought forth fruit, then appeared the tares also. So the servants of the householder came and said unto him, Sir, didst not thou sow good seed in thy field? from whence then hath it tares? He said unto them, An enemy hath done this. The servants said unto him, Wilt thou then that we go and gather them up? But he said, Nay; lest while ye gather up the tares, ye root up also the wheat with them.

Let both grow together until the harvest: and in the time of harvest I will say to the reapers, Gather ye together first the tares, and bind them in bundles to burn them: but gather the wheat into my barn." [10]

It is interesting to note that Jesus indicated that the servant was not to pull out the tares until the right time. What are they doing there? He said if they are pulled out prematurely the wheat will go with them. This is a brilliant insight. By analogy tares are an antecedent for the wheat. They are a type of "trigger" that says, "There is still something in the wheat that needs to be dealt with." We don't readily see this because we all would like to see the tares gone. They are sharp, course, pointed and irritating, but in some cases they represent assignments; difficult but they have a purpose. *Charles. R Swindoll writes:*

"There are no problems quite like people problems, are there? You can have a job that demands

long hours and great physical effort, but neither the hours nor the energy drain gives you the problems difficult people do. You can have financial difficulties, physical pain, a tight schedule, and miles of driving, but these things are not the cause of our major battles. It's people; ...The grind of difficult people is quite an assignment!" [11]

Let's say that throughout our lives we encounter only nice people; people that are honest, gentle, kind, pleasant and so forth—those who don't cause any difficulties whatsoever. How would we really know how we would behave in adverse circumstances? It is the difficult people that show us who we really are. Or should I say, it is our reaction to their negative behaviour that shows us who we really are.

Material possessions may be the result of our hard work. They reveal what we have. Adversities and our ability to work gently, systematically and methodically with the difficult people and situations reveal who we truly are. Unfortunately, our society has chosen to view possessions as being the bench-mark of success. In many cases this is why good behaviour is at a premium. Godly behaviour is not highly valued. The ***crisis: identity*** will continue until we come to the place where we identify ourselves the way God identifies us, as being *in His own image and likeness*. The image of God in us is the potential for excellence and yet some behave as though we are not connected to God. However it is in healthy relationships that we have the opportunity to develop excellent character; this gives credence to the saying *"No man is an island."*

As we continue to grow and develop here is another strategy that can be implemented to help us when we face challenging people and situations.

Model # 2

"R-R-S-P"

Recognize	Respond	Support	Pray

RRSP stands for Recognize, Respond, Support and Pray. When we feel that we are in a crisis situation, we need to recognize it for what it is, but more importantly we need to recognize our mental, emotional and physical state. This in place we can arm ourselves with R-R-S-P to deal with the situation in an appropriate manner. The reason for this is we must have congruency in ourselves. Head and heart (thoughts and feelings) must be in agreement. We can then respond appropriately instead of reacting. Following this we need to give ourselves support, assuring ourselves that our intentions and motives for responding are pure and Godly. Then we call for *backup* from God. This works every time if we follow it properly. Some say, "Why don't you call for back-up first?" It is perfectly fine to do so. I have found that, because God is always with us, it goes without saying. He is in command. We should be in constant communication with Him. Therefore; in crisis I need to make sure that I am aware of my own attitude. Calling on God is an on-going thing, before, during and after a crisis.

Crisis: identity plagues the whole world because, in a nutshell, we have deteriorated spiritually to the point where we don't really know who we are. It is like going to the bank to draw out money without having an account. When one has a bank account (under normal conditions) he has a right to his money as long as he can identify himself to the bank. God has given an account to every person and that account is wrapped up in the identity of personhood whether we believe it or not. God said that He made man in His image. He did not say that He made Christians in His image. He made all people in His image and likeness. He made us with a great wealth of potential in our account.

The day that God revealed this to me, it was so exciting. I remember thinking, "No one is born a Christian." All humans come into the world with the potential for greatness and goodness. When we ask the Lord to come into our lives and become followers of Christ, this is a bonus. Can you imagine! Even before coming into the reality of friendship with God I have the potential of Godliness in me. His image is there. His potential is in us and in this reality we have all been given the *right* to develop ourselves to the highest degree. It is with His help that we are able to do this. Potential to show real love is what Jesus spelled out in the saying "By this shall all men know that you are my disciple if you have love for one another."[12] Many struggle to do this using their own abilities when only God's Spirit can do this work in us.

The image of God in us is our identity card and our potential for a celebrative life. This is safety. If God is in us and God is love then we have the potential to love as He loves. Without this acknowledgement and understanding we are not safe people. It's no wonder the church is struggling to bring the world to God when all along God wants to bring the world to Himself through His children, not through dinners, bake sales, movies, seminars, conventions and rallies, but through our Godly behaviour and attitude. If we change our attitude and behaviour to reflect Jesus the world will respond to God in a positive way because they are waiting to experience God through interacting with those who call themselves Christians.

The world has seen so much phoniness, hypocrisy and negativity from so called Christians who have turned off many to the point where they are scared of going to church. As a matter of fact, I have seen more admirably behaviours in dealing with some who do not call themselves Christians than with some church folks. The bottom line is that negative behaviours of Christians are keeping the world out of the church. Why should they come into the church's mess when they have seen enough mess in the world?

A few years ago I stood on the doorstep of a notoriously famous church with a distressed sixteen year old boy whose life hung in the balance. As he struggled with drugs and family crisis, I listened to his painful story with a desire to help him. The moment of intense healing was shattered as two irate older Christians emerged from the basement of the church ready to swing blows at each other. Moving from shock to denial at what I was witnessing, I instantly tried to shelter the distressed young man from what quickly appeared to be a scene that had the potential of becoming a Mohamed Ali and Joe Fraser bout. I gave much thanks to God as one of them escaped to their car and left the scene dropping these words "I don't think there is enough room in this church for both of us." With that the car door slammed. I think this is quite serious, not only because this kind of behaviour has happened often, but because it is still happening among Christians.

I have tried to chuck this up to just human behaviour, but the reality is, since we grow physically do we not want to grow spiritually and emotionally as well? Why is it when there is a problem we use the same negative emotions (i.e. anger, frustration, bitterness, etc.) that we used when we were five years old?

There are times when I have had to chuckle as I go to some special service and understand that the idea behind having that service is to draw in the 'unbeliever.' When I look around, all I see are believers. I ask myself, "Where are the ones that we are praying for?" The answer came to me very clearly one day while I was on my face before the throne of grace, crying out to the Lord. He spoke to me and told me that we are wasting our time because, until we decide to love one another as He commanded in the New Testament, we are not going to move forward. This love will cause us to have Godly behaviour and it is that Godly behaviour that enables us to move forward.

The early New Testament church operated in the Spirit and in New Testament type of love. They were also familiar with Holy Spirit and listened to Him. They listened to Him and were led by Him. Many Christians today operate on a different level. They make plans and then ask God to bless them. I have noticed that when God asks us to do something it automatically carries His blessings. The reason that some of us struggle so much in our walk with the Lord is because, for the most part, we don't take the time to *know* Holy Spirit and to hear what He (the voice of God on the earth) is saying. In addition to this, we do not train ourselves to behave in ways that attract the world and reflect God's image in us. We all understand that serving God is a journey and a process; however, training is needed from the day we accept Christ in our lives to help us learn to do what God desires. Seeking God, listening to His voice and obeying Him qualifies us to call ourselves Christians. To be led by Holy Spirit is the key to success and to becoming a safe person.

We will continue to put millions of dollars into buildings and programs and waste monies that could be used to feed the poor in the world until we decide to change our behaviour, do what Jesus said, and begin to love, not in the Old Testament way, but in the New Testament way, which is to love one another as Jesus has loved us.

Some churches are not safe, many homes (even Christian homes) are not safe, and we can see that the world is not safe. Where then do we find safety?

It is difficult to embrace the love of God, and to love as God loves until we learn to love ourselves as God does. Many of us are not able to look in the mirror and love our *selves* because there is so much pain. This is why so many people do not stay in themselves. It is not a safe place to be. People say that they can love another person but they can't love themselves. This is not possible. Let's look at this logically. The first premise is that love for our neighbour is based on love for self. This means the same love that I have for myself is what I have for my neighbour. Premise two, on a scale of 1-10 if all the love that I can give to self is 1 or 2, then that is all I am capable of giving to my neighbour. This is very simple to understand if we can understand that the word "*as*" means the same. Having the love for self that is appropriate sets us in the right position to show care and compassion to others. <u>John Bradshaw writes;</u>

> *"For me one of the most significant consequences of imaginatively embracing my inner child was that it gave me a way to be compassionate with myself. When I look in the mirror, even now, the old voices of blame, comparison, and self contempt start playing. Even after years of hearing new voices in my friendships and community fellowship, I can hear those old posthypnotic tapes. For years I read books that offered techniques to help one love oneself. I stared in the mirror and said, "I love you, John," over and over. It helped for a few minutes and then the voices just got worse.*
>
> *... One day I closed my eyes and saw a little boy. His picture is now inside the back cover of the paperback version of Homecoming. I felt immediate love for him. He was standing on the front porch of a house on Fannin Street in Houston, Texas. This was the house where I was born. He was resting his chin on cupped hands and gazing out in wonder at the world. I felt so much love I began to cry softly. I couldn't believe the depth of emotion. My soul was at it again! As I embraced this image of myself as a boy, I embraced myself. It was powerful and transformative. I loved myself in this image of a boy. Through him I could accept myself unconditionally."[13]*

A lady once told me that she was totally unable to look at herself in the mirror and like what she saw. Upon investigation of her past, we discovered that there were some negative issues that were still holding her captive. After a few months of sharing our life's stories she was able to gradually begin to look at herself in the mirror with a greater level of comfort and compassion.

Many people, including believers in God, have a very difficult time with self-love. I have encouraged several people to love themselves because this will help them to develop a sense of who they are and promote a healthy level of Godly self-care. I was taken aback when I realized the number of people that confused self-love with selfishness. It was amazing! I have heard it all. They say, "Oh, but we must not be selfish; we must not put too much emphasis on self."

Some say, "Did the Bible not say that we must be humble?" Or, "We must put others first." The list goes on. All of this is said in an effort to not put self in the picture. What I have also discovered is that because so much emphasis has been put on denying self, self becomes lost. When self is loved the way that God intended it to be, we don't struggle with pride and self-interest because Godly self-love gives us a sense of belonging. It is because *self* is crying out for love that we struggle with things such as selfishness, fear, anger, self-interest and pride. It simply means that we are not feeling safe and loved within ourselves. As a result we become toxic. We will have no problem taking care of our neighbour when self-care and self-love are in place.

Feeling safe absolutely begins with love for self. Being able to connect and show real compassion for ourselves indeed is fulfillment in life. Sadly, many of us grew up in dysfunctional homes without the ability to protect ourselves. As a result, we developed what some people call a *false self*, or a *fictional self*. I will call it the *phantom-self*. This is the self that came into being to help us bare the pain when we were being abused (in whatever way). This phantom-self carries all the images and emotional data from the past and does not go away when we grow up physically. It stays with us all the time and when we face challenges we behave the same way we did when we were children because the information data base from the past is still there. In other words, the abused state that has been recorded in our sub-conscious from the past carries the emotional information to the present situation. This data is so clear in the sub-conscious that it is as if it were happening in the present. Each time we face a challenge we draw up the old emotional information and images and exhibit the corresponding behaviour. Relief can come from prayer and I do know that prayer works. It must not be discounted. However, *God moves in mysterious ways and He* is able to work through other means if we trust Him. I have watched many people struggle with inner pain for years; even those who call themselves Christians. Some that are in pain will say that there is no need to go back to the past to find out where they were hurt. "We are saved," They say. "Just pray and things will be fine." Then as time goes on, because they have not dealt with their inner pain, they continue to have bad behaviours, even when they reach old age. This is due to the cry of their souls that are still in pain. I believe that, because we are spirit, we have souls and we live in bodies. If we neglect any part of this human dynamic we will do ourselves a disservice.

The pain on the inside is in the soul and some people have been able to bury it very deep in order to not show who they really are, but they can't always hide the corresponding emotional information. Therefore, when a crisis comes, the truth of their inner pain is revealed and their behaviour shows it. Learning to love self God's way will eventually result in feeling safe enough to develop healthy boundaries. That will constantly make us aware of our personal environment. Personal love and safety will result in us having safe homes, churches, schools and our communities.

Model three will help to put things in perspective. As mentioned God uses other means along with prayer to help in our healing processes; among those that have helped me in my life is one that I will called ***superimposing or fading.***

Model # 3

Superimposition Therapy or Fading

Another healing tool that has worked for me I have called ***Superimposition therapy***. As mentioned before damaging images and feelings from the past have inter-fered with the inner space causing us to respond to life's challenges in inappropriate ways. These images, emotional data and behaviours will be there until they are over taken or weakened by stronger and more powerful images and positive information. For example, if one desires to remove her past abusers, she will have to design a mental image like Jesus or an angel helping her remove the past images. She[41] can choose whatever hero image she desires but the key is that she needs to do it herself. If it is done for her it will not work as well. The reason for this is, in doing this routine the individual gains back her personal power that was stolen when she was abused. A therapist can walk through this process with her, but the effectiveness of the procedure comes when the abused person actually sees herself personally removing her abusers. This action helps the individual's personal power to be restored and causes the old images to slowly fade. The corresponding ***emotional pain and* data** will eventually fade as well. For the most part, when children were being abused they lost a sense of self and become powerless. This action restores their power and causes self to begin feeling healthy.

Model # 4

Remember that emotions were with us before we could talk. For example, as babies, we laugh, we cry etc. Our emotions are in the original human *bar-code;* they are stamped deep in the sub-conscious. We all came in the world with an original *barcode* given by God. It contains all the information on the blessings, promises and intentions of God for us and, believe it or not, there is not one negative thought or word in it.

Human Bar Code

GRACE

LOVE

MERCY

POWER

PEACE

CHARING

CHERISH

This example shows a few of the qualities coded in the original human bar code.

The Lord showed this to me and I was so honoured. ***The human bar code*** is similar to the commercial bar-code that is usually on the bottom or the side of products that carries information relating to the product. The difference is the ***human bar code*** records information and messages from care-givers early in life that can last a life-time. The code is in our sub-conscious and it also has the image of God imbedded in it...His likeness is deep in the code. If we can take a hold of this, it has the potential to change our lives for good. It will cause us to become ***response-able*** instead of being ***reactors***. As adults, it will also help us to see the tremendous task of raising children and preparing them for a successful life by investing positive things in them. When positive things are put in the code positive behaviours will eventually result. Our feelings are constantly being scanned on the *bar-code*. When our hearts picks up something that triggers it, we know, because we feel it. If it is in the code and is positive, we respond positively. If it is negative and it connects to our belief about ourselves, we react negatively.

Here is how it works. Let's say an adult is called a bad name, perhaps *jerk*. The name *jerk* is scanned on the **bar code** in the sub-conscious and that name did not pick up any emotional pain so the person will not feel this word. Neither will they react to it. It is not in their code system. However, if the name causes some feeling (negative emotion) that triggers a negative behaviour, it means that the name has been scanned on the ***human bar code*** and that name *jerk* has picked up the corresponding pain information that is associated with it.

If we had negative messages from care-givers such as, "you are stupid and you won't amount to anything," *jerk* and the like, these messages cause confusion and hinder progress in the lives of many people. But we must remember that these negative messages were <u>put in</u> the code system they are not a part of the original code. Therefore, while they cannot be erased they can be diminished by emphasizing what God has said about us. Also, superimposing stronger images will help to fade those negative codes, especially in cases where abuse took place. Knowing what God has said about us is paramount to our success in this life.

Biblical writers:

> *"For unto the angels hath He not put in subjection the world to come, whereof we speak? But one in a certain place testified, saying, what is man, that thou art mindful of him? or the son of man that thou visitest him? Thou madest him a little lower than the angels; thou crownest him with glory and honour, and didst set him over the works of thy hands: Thou hast put all things in subjection under his feet. For in that He put all in subjection under him, he left nothing that is not put under him. But now we see not yet all things put under him."[14]*

> *"For thou hast possessed my reins: thou hast covered me in my mother's womb. I will praise thee; for I am fearfully and wonderfully made: marvellous are thy works; and that my soul knoweth right well. My substance was not hid from thee, when I was made in secret, and curiously wrought in the lowest part of the earth. Thine eyes did see my substance, yet being unperfect; and in thy book all my members were written, which in continuance were fashioned, when as yet there was none of them."[15]*

The information given by the care-givers remains in the phantom-self and the information from God are in the real-self. Depending on the self- training that has taken place, the individual will revert to the care-givers database in times of crisis because that is the familiar territory. This is the reason that we desperately need to override the old images and information with stronger images of God's Word, self-love and compassion. This will cause us to gradually relinquish the old and painful self (phantom-self).

It is also important to remove ourselves from people who insist on telling us that "we are our worst enemy." This is a lie, and can become a prevention of self-growth. What can be more damaging than for our human spirit, to hear that we are our worst enemy? Talk about devastating!

The adult's emotional data base is full of information from childhood. We tend to behave in the same ways as we did when we were children unless we over-ride the negative images and emotions therapeutically, as previously mentioned. If we chose not to believe this, then take a look at the behaviour of an angry adult. For example, something happens and they did not get what they wanted; sometimes the behaviour can be very negative ranging from sulking to angry words, to violence. This kind of behaviour is telling the individual that there is pain in the soul. Just the same way that physical pain tells us that there is something wrong in the body, emotional pain is generally a "messenger" telling us that there is something wrong in the soul. The soul and body were engineered to be governed by the spirit. Not dealing with childhood abuse hinders the development of the soul. If parents spend half the time developing the child's soul as they do the body they would experience less negative behaviours. The soul is mind, will and emotion and the spirit is the God's-image connection. Abuses and corresponding pain information from the past hinders us from staying at **home**, **home** being the safe-space inside our selves. When danger such as abuse is present we leave because the pain is too difficult to manage.

Being at **home** emotionally, spiritually and personally also means feeling safe. Our personal "homeostasis" must be in place. In other words, the thermostat of the inner-person must be at the right temperature (feeling loved). Nothing will put it there and keep it there as much as love for God and for one*self*. The more we love ourselves the more we love God. I know that some people will be offended at this statement because they were taught to love God first, and here lies the dilemma. They say that they love God because that is what they are taught, yet they continue to struggle with their own self-love, not to mention loving others. Why? Remember God said *"thou shalt have no other gods before me" "love neighbour as self"* and *"love one another as He loves us.* "Trying" to do any of these commandments puts us in a category of disobedience. Surprise! The ability to do them is not up to our "trying" it is up to our "yielding" to His Spirit. Think of the image of a cross. It is both horizontal and vertical. The vertical part can be put in the ground and be made to stand up, but the horizontal needs the vertical to hold it up. Case in point, God is the vertical, and we are the horizontal. The same principal applies to self-love. If we "try" to love God that is all we are doing, "trying." Allowing God through His Spirit to love through us causes us to love Him first, then self and others. Here is truth manifested.

God is love; this love must be manifested in us by God. This is the "ID" (Identity Card) that self is looking for. This ends **_crisis: identity_**. Applying Model # 5 for feeling safe can be a part of our healing.

Model # 5

Model for feeling safe

1. Surround yourself with emotionally safe people; those who do not use negative emotions to work through life's difficulties.

2. Choose your close friends carefully; have only a few friends that want the best for you.

3. Do not carry other people's baggage (their personal problems)

4. Document all your negative behaviours, they are messengers from the past; then deal with them

5. If you choose to carry the baggage of others do it without complaining; you chose to do it.

6. Make a decision to love yourself, once you make that decision, watch how much better you feel.

7. Never do anything without your mind and heart in union; otherwise this is "emotional rape."

Chapter 3

Running From Home

I have heard it said often that *"home is where the heart is."* If that is true, it presupposes that home is a place of comfort, and the heart likes to feel at home. However, many people live with a sense of fear of being by themselves in their own hearts. Others are not able to be quiet because of the terror of being alone. I have seen people who are dedicated to abusive relationships, because they are not able to be alone. We must ask ourselves, what hinders us from being comfortable within ourselves? It could be that the feeling of comfort has gone from our hearts causing us to vacate them.

There are a number of things that transpire over our lifetime that makes it difficult for some of us to feel comfortable within ourselves. Childhood rejection, broken relationships, etcetera; these difficulties tend to diminish a healthy sense of self. One of the reasons that we find it difficult to accept and stay within ourselves as adults is, because we are living under a cloud of shame. We are using shame as a whip to beat ourselves to where we feel that we have paid for all the wrongs that we have done. Because God did not intend this kind of punishment for us our hearts can never accept this kind of reasoning. I have outlined the meaning of self acronymicly;

S- Satisfied; E- enjoyable; L-lovable; F- fulfilled.

Self-satisfaction may sound as though it is self-glorying. On the contrary; what it is means is an affirmation, accommodation and a welcoming of one's self. The acceptance of self is one of the four foundational posts (if you like) of stability in all human life. Satisfied with who we are becomes fundamental to knowing our true potential and helps us in our development on all levels. The four pillars for growth and stability are; acceptance, affection, attention and approval.

Enjoyable is the sense of comfort and pleasure in us and toward God. Love toward self is also a personal stabilizer. Being fulfilled as God intended is a sense of being completed in God; it's a sense of completeness as we recognize that we are here for God's glory. Let's observe these words one by one.

S = Satisfied

Not often do we meet people who will be satisfied with themselves. They are either too fat, skinny or too "something else." In our Western society body-image has captured the minds of many. We invest millions of dollars on looking good physically. Exercise equipment and products to keep us trim are selling like hot-cakes but, in spite of this, people are still struggling with personal satisfaction. The reason is that they are not **home**. "At **home**" means that we are comfortable with ourselves. Many of the dissatisfaction that we experience is not just about body-image. It is attached to the deep dissatisfaction on the inside, the inner person or the image of self has been marred.

People spend so much time and money working on the body that the spirit and soul tends to be neglected. The benefits of exercise and a good diet are enormous and should never be discounted, but we need a balance. During the years when I was not in school I was very dedicated to a regimental exercise program and I was able to keep the weight at bay. This was a part of my plan to keep my life in control.

Many are so driven by their heavily scheduled lifestyle that it becomes challenging to even take the time to pray and relax. Our appetite for affluence and success has also become a growing concern. It seems that our lives are out of control. How do we strike a balance? *Bob Shank writes:*

> *"After one remarkable day during which He healed many and gave powerful words of encouragement, He refused to heed the popular cry to spend more time with this adoring crowd. Why? He told His followers He had other villages to visit and other people to whom He had to preach. "That is why I have come" he said. He knew His purpose in life, and He didn't let popular opinion sway Him from His course.*
>
> *We know, of course, that this man was Jesus Christ—the most incredible example of control the world has ever seen. He provides a benchmark against which to measure ourselves."[16]*

Distractions are so strong in our society that they have the potential to suck even the most vigilant and purpose driven people into lives of constant achieving and running, yet they never get to the place of true self-satisfaction. This constant achieving is called performance and indicates a lack of self-approval. It can keep some people on a treadmill to a point where they are not able to leave their work at the workplace, causing a more stressful life. Separating work from the rest of our lives is a recommendation from *Richard Carlson, Ph.D. He writes:*

> *"There are few things more predictable than the stress you create for yourself when you fail to separate your work from the rest of your life. I don't mean you shouldn't work at home, only that you should take steps toward separating your work from the rest of your life"*[17]

In a society where home has become an office, how do we find peace and tranquility in the inner resources of the human heart? Home is a place to relax, reflect and find repose. The idea of home being a place where peace and comfort prevails is the order of the day but it is becoming a thing of the past because so many have had to leave **home** (the inner space) due to personal Tsunamis and Katrinas. When these things happen they cause some to run from *home.*

They ran for their lives taking nothing with them. This seems the safest thing to do in a time of crisis. To mention returning *home* to some people conjures up fear and sad memories, and presents them with another trauma of, "how do I face it?" I have met many people that are outside their *home;* and their behaviours show it. Here are a few of them: anger, insecurity, judgmental attitude, low self image, gossip and control. There are more but these top the list. These negative behaviours are used by the "homeless" as deflectors. They are used to keep intruders out. They have been used by those that have been hurt over a period of time to get attention to the point where they now use them automatically. Think for a moment. If a burglar enters someone's house in the middle of the night and they are alone, the first thing that will go through that person's mind is "how do I get out alive. They may try to throw something at the intruder or scream in order to scare off the intruder. Hurting people are scared and will use negative behaviours to "ward off" those that they see as threats. When one is outside their _home_ the result is the use of negative behaviours....and anger is the most frequently used emotion, because it is the one that reflects power and control. At some point in this person's life intruders came in and caused some damage and they have become the victim that was never vindicated. However, the Bible encourages the proper use of anger, *William Backus & Marie Chapian writes:*

> *"Anger is not always bad. On the contrary, anger can be normal and has adaptive significance in appropriate situations. Remember, Jesus experienced anger. The simple emotion of anger is not always harmful or unloving. It is what you do when you are angry that has moral significance. Paul wrote, "Be angry, and yet do not sin; do not let the sun go down on your anger." The Amplified version of this verse reads, "When angry do not sin," which surely indicates we may sometimes feel angry. Paul is telling us that anger in itself is not wicked; that what we do when angry can be sinful; and that we should not allow ourselves to remain angry by continuing our destructive, resentful self-talk."[18]*

It is not possible to have a healthy relationship with those that we are afraid of and destructive angry behaviour has the tendency to repel people making it difficult to establish healthy relationships.

Insecurity is another behaviour that works as a deflector; it has the classic ability to cripple the building of secure friendships. It is like a watchtower with its lights burnt out. The boats are coming and someone was neglectful in replacing the light-bulbs. Dangerous! You bet!

Judgmental behaviour is one of the most damaging; both to the one who does it and the recipient. It is dangerous because it presupposes that we can see inside someone's heart and, as far as I know, only God can know someone's heart. I recall many years ago I was working in a secular job. The gossip was painful to say the very least. Every day I cringed in my heart as I thought of going to the dining room table and listening as certain workers were put through the "shredder." I took it for a while but then I thought, "If I listen to it, I am a part of it." After prayer, I received the courage of my conviction to speak up—and speak up I did. One day they were gossiping about a certain person and I asked if anyone had gone to this person's face to talk to her. Silence fell like a thick, wet blanket over the table. Heads dropped and chins were now scraping the floor. I continued, "Maybe, if she knew what is being said here at this table, she may have an opportunity to speak for herself and possibly change her behaviour." The silence prevailed as one by one they crawled away from the table. Shoulders shrugged and eyes bulged. Needless to say, I was treated in a different way after that day. Not too many rushed to sit beside me at the table, which in some ways worked to my advantage as I did not have to listen to trash. I knew that Jesus in me was not comfortable listening to that gossip anyway. I also discovered later on, when I worked with the same person that was being criticized, that all that was being said about her was a result of crisis in her home which no one knew about. The point here is, when we look at another human being we may see them smiling, or not. They may demonstrate certain behaviours, or not. The only safe thing to do is to leave our *"gavel"* at the cross of Jesus. That is all that is safe and necessary to do because if we judge it will return to us or our families eventually. What we can do, however, is to pray for them. If we criticize, analyze, judge or speculate we have gone too far and we are on dangerous grounds. I once asked a lady who seemed to have had a Masters degree in gossip if she thought that she could just admire another person on the basis that they are God's creation. "Just leave it there and have no negative thoughts about her," I suggested. She said "No!" Tearing other people apart is a learned behaviour. Not tearing them apart is also a learned behaviour and a very rewarding one. It creates a sense of cleanness on the inside. I am totally shocked at the amount of gossip and criticism among those that call themselves Christian. This is vicious, devilish and damming, to say the least. I believe the reason for this could be that many people suffer from low, or no self image and they develop a false sense of self by putting other people down because they are not ___home___ or safe within themselves.

Low self image is directly linked to the lack of understanding about the healthy Godly image and is seen frequently in the ___homeless___. To break the pattern of low self-image one needs to admit that they do have this problem and understand that they are worthy of all God's best. If they are not able to see this they will remain "stuck." To be "stuck" means being helpless and helpless people behave helplessly. They are always down on themselves and others, behaving negatively and are emotionally bankrupt.

It is like coming to a crossroad of decision making in one's mind and hearing several voices shouting from every corner, "This is the right way." Confusion would only begin to express that state of mind. Being "stuck" is like this. It can be paralyzing.

I will deal a little more with self-esteem because it is the root-system of many of the issues that we deal with on a daily basis and the symptoms are jealousy, anger, fear, resentment, racism and prejudices, to name a few. Not having the kind of self-esteem that was intended by God is more than just being a problem. It is a disaster. It is a great source of stress, anxiety and conflict in every society. If we were to begin to deal with most of the problems in the world, we would find out that self-esteem issues are at the very root of them. Trying to fix the problems of the world without dealing with self- rejection issues is like "putting the cart before the horse" The reason for this is, people who suffer from self-esteem issues have no real "God-image" of themselves (this is dangerous). Consequently they are like "chaff" to the winds of life; blown in every direction. It takes time and determination to develop a real self concept especially when ideas about self formed in childhood were damaged, *Cecil Osborne explains:*

> *"The conscious and unconscious feelings you have about yourself constitute your self-image. This self-image you will act out in life. You will always tend to act in harmony with it.*
>
> *The Bible recognizes this. The author of Proverbs writes, 'For as he thinketh in his heart, so is he.' When the Bible uses the term heart it is referring to the emotions, among other things, 'the centre of our being.' Modern psychology confirms the insight*

of Proverbs: Whatever you feel yourself to be at the centre of your emotional nature, that is what you really are, existentially, and your actions will be in harmony with your self-concept."[19]

To unravel the mystery of trying to serve God as we have been taught; working in the community, helping the lonely and the poor without a clear experience with the God-image (self-image) in us is truly paradoxical. Jesus said *"the kingdom of God is within you"* This being the "ID" card of connection with Him begs the question, what are we working from, if self-image is not in place?

When Jesus came to the crippled man at the pool of Bethesda who was there for thirty eight years, He asked him, *"Wilt thou be made whole?* Jesus knew that this man was crippled in more places than his body. His self-image had been shattered. It was his confession that held him captive. He said to Jesus, "Sir, I have no man, when the water is troubled to put me into the pool: but while I am coming, another steppeth down before me". "Having no man" is the thing that prevented him from the power of the healing waters. *"Having no man" explains his depleted self-image.* We teach others how to treat us. His crippled emotions and self-esteem told others to leave him there. They did; for thirty eight years.

Conversely, it seems to me that word would have gotten around that this man needed "a turn" to get to the water; and after thirty eight years someone would have had some compassion and helped him into the water. Common sense says it would be very unlikely that it was his parents who brought him there and abandoned him. The other thought is, if his friends brought him, somebody would have stayed to help him until the troubling of the water. Could this man have been a loner, a derelict, possibly a foreigner (the untouchable?) The story does not say. The busy sheep market of Bethesda and the scrambling of sick bodies to get to a pool for healing makes an interesting back-drop for the drama of a broken man's life. Diseased in so many outstanding ways he drew the immediate attention of Jesus to him above the others that were there waiting.

How often do we put our lives in reverse due to our lack of self- awareness and our God-given potential? Fear is one of the hindrances that hold us from doing what God has called us to do. We think that we are not capable and sometimes we worry about being in His will; but when we are surrendered to God, His will works in us and He blesses whatever He possesses.

There is always hope and help in God and, through prayer, Holy Spirit (God's agent on the earth) will guide us to work with God as He works with us. *Cecil Osborne explains;*

> *"With the conscious mind one may settle on some desirable goal. It may be the securing of an education, the ability to make friends, a personality change, or even a material possession. This is determined by the conscious mind and is the result of our ambitions, desires, and sense of values. ...*
>
> *However, the universe is so geared as to aid us in reaching worthy and creative goals. 'The stars in their courses' are on the side of one who dares to dream great dreams if they are consistent with God's will.*
>
> *It is only as we spend time in honest soul-searching in the presence of God that we dare to dream these great dreams and ask Him to help us*

attain them. ...God is at work within you, both to will and to work for His good pleasure."[20]

Another problem is controlling people. They can be the most difficult to deal with because they tend to play God. They have a need to do everything and to know everything. The controller goes through the painful task of manipulating life's circumstances to have it go their way. The problem is that they are not always aware that they are trying to control everything and will blame others for having controlling behaviours.

Those who demonstrate these behaviours are definitely not at *home*. The question is how do we help them to return? First, we need to find out what drove them from their **homes**. It could be the tsunami of a dysfunctional family, it could be the hurricane of a shattered marriage or it could be the devastation of the loss of a loved one. There are so many reasons why folks leave *home.* To help the controller return *home* one must become a safe person. The main issue of controlling people is called insecurity. They are also vulnerable, scared and very sensitive. They will need people who care from the heart to walk them back *home.* We need to understand that compassion is connected to God's heart and cannot be faked. Compassion is not feeling sorry for someone. It means fostering pro-active change. It is not possible to care from the heart without a true desire to bring about positive change in the situation. This means that we are tuned into God, able to feel His heart, communicate His passion and change negative circumstances to positive. Being real, as Jesus was to the people that He ministered to, is very important. Those that are in pain have developed a great sensitivity to that which is real and that which is phony; they know the difference.

We must be real in our care of others it is a key to their healing process. Our hearts must be in whatever care we give and if this care is from the heart it means that we are safe people.

Becoming a safe person will require us to have the heart of Jesus. He was moved with compassion when He saw the pain of the wandering multitude. To have the heart of Jesus one must come face to face with God then we will be able to come heart to heart with the pain of the hurting, not necessarily physically experiencing what they are feeling, but understanding what they are going through. Remember, a Doctor doesn't have to have cancer in order to treat a cancer patient, but he will have to know the proper amount of medication to administer to the patients in order to not hurt them. Understanding means that we are able to "go where they are" and be present and empathetic. We may face obstacles as we do this. But the determination and sincerity of our heats will bring good results. The Syrophenician woman who came to Jesus seeking help for her demonized daughter faced many obstacles right off the bat. She was chased by the disciples, called a dog by Jesus plus she knew her status of being "less." The key to this whole story is the fact that brokenness on the part of any human always moves the heart of the Father. Always! This woman came to Jesus fully aware that all she was entitled to were the "crumbs" that fell from the table, but she refused to allow that to be an obstacle. Jesus himself knew the meaning of "crumbs from the table." The power of humility and brokenness was overwhelming for them both. It melted their hearts into inner bonding. Regardless of all the obstacles, she felt connected with the Lord and did not allow the exterior issues to disturb the "inner connection" that was made between them. In this connection the hurting finds safety. The hurting will continue to die in their pain if they feel any "superior" attitude from those who try to help them.

Crumbs under the table also speak of bending down. It is not a "table meal." It is eaten off the floor, lowly and in pieces. God connects with the lowly and the weak and I can hear the voice of Jesus saying to this broken woman, "I too will be broken for you. I feel your hurt and your faith has saved your daughter. I am the crumbs—the broken bread—take—eat." Fantastic! "Identification" took place and this is the connection that must happen in us as well in order to bring the wounded and *__homeless__* back *__home__*.

We must eliminate all criticism and judgment from our hearts. The Father's heart is full (not half-full) of compassion, not criticism. David knew all about this. He explains:

> *"The Lord is gracious and full of compassion;*
> *slow to anger and of great mercy. The Lord is good*
> *to all: and His tender mercies are over all His*
> *works."*[21]

As mentioned earlier, the church is struggling to bring the hurting ones in. Some bring them by feeding them. Feeding them is good but, if the real Christ-like compassion is not shown, all we are doing is feeding the physical. The inner-brokenness will continue. Remember, the Lord is full of compassion. When we are full of compassion, there is no room for tearing down those that are already wounded. So often we try to help others but we find room in our hearts for blame and shame by telling them that their situation is their fault and then we set out on a campaign to fix them. Hurting people are not in need of being fixed. They need a friend, a confidant, someone who understands and someone who is not ashamed to walk along-side them; especially those living with a sense of being cheated, neglected, marginalized or robbed. Those experiencing divorce (which by the way is treated as the unpardonable sin by some churches), whose dreams have been shattered, are lost and are seen as "second class citizens" are desperately in need of care. Antoinette Bosco explains:

> *"I think for all of us there was first the sense of being cheated. We had begun our young adult years with great expectations. Certainly we had entered our marriages believing that we would live happily ever after—for life. But our great expectations were shattered and we had to learn as Margaret Mitchell expresses in <u>Gone With the Wind</u>, 'Life is under no obligation to give us what we expect'*
> *Then we all had to deal with a changed self-image and cope with it. This certainly involves not only how we view ourselves but also how others—like family, neighbours, church, etc., view us."* [22]

When someone encounters an accident and finds herself in a hospital where she should get help, does the attending physician scold her for having a wound, a broken bone or an illness? No! Treatment is given with the goal of the person getting better. Then how is it that the broken and wounded of our churches come under such heavy criticism, judgment and ridicule? I have said so often that the church is a hospital. It is a place for those that are hurting to get the help they need in order to get well. The church of Jesus Christ should be the safest place on the earth for everyone, especially the wounded, but sadly it is not. This must change— and quickly. The "powers that be" must by all means do something to put an end to the abuses that are taking place in the churches. Absolutely no one would stand by passively and watch abuses happen in any public hospital and do nothing about it. The time has come to take a stand to eradicate the evil of politics, gossip, judgments and criticism from the body of Christ and replace them with the true New Testament commandment to love one another as Christ loves. I have been totally amazed at the number of Christians who are still living under the Old Testament mentality of loving neighbour as self. I realize that Jesus spoke about this kind of love before He went to the cross just as He spoke of loving one another as "He loves." But because He has finished the work of redemption through His death on the cross, all we need to do now is to surrender our whole heart to Him. He wants to live His life in us so that we can end the struggle of trying to love. Loving as He loves brings us into oneness.

> *"That they all may be one; as thou, Father, art in me, and I in thee, that they also may be one in us: that the world may believe that thou hast sent me."*[23]

To experience this "oneness" that Jesus so eloquently spoke about, it must happen in self first, then with God, before it can happen with the neighbour. I have seen so many in the churches pray for "oneness" until they are about to turn green. I have seen the programs and the money that has been spent to promote church unity. It is done with a belief that God is going to do what He has asked us to do. NO! This "oneness" is the connecting of Hearts, ours and God's through His Son Jesus Christ.

Our clicks are causing many who need the love of God to stay away; when they come and feel our rejection, they don't return.

For many years I attended a Pentecostal church in the city of London, Ontario that was predominantly white. I was among the few adventurous blacks that dared to venture in—but venture in—I did. I watched as a certain black family sat in the same place each Sunday morning. The music was loud and sometimes bothersome but I was able to handle that far more than the blatant discrimination that I saw as family after family and person after person would skirt around this particular family, in order to not get close to them. It was horrible! Yet, the songs of "loving God" echoed loud and clear. Hands were raised in adoration to the One whose heart cries out and sincerely prays for "oneness". "Oneness," did you say? It pained me to the core.

Everything that God created relates to Him, and humans are His "feature presentation." In us exits the pre-existing pattern for "oneness" with God and one another. All we need to do is submit to it and allow Holy Spirit to work it through us. This is not rocket science but it is a type of science that will rocket us into the empty space in our hearts called our ***home; where true love begins.***

E= Enjoyable

Begin to tell yourself that you are an enjoyable person and just see how it feels. Awkward! It took me many years before I could give mental assent to the Biblical account that God made us for His pleasure and glory and that He enjoys and desires us to enjoy Him. Revelation speaks to this reality.

> *"Thou art worthy, O Lord, to receive glory and honour and power: for thou hast created all things, and for thy pleasure they are and were created."*[24]

The Greek meaning of this Word pleasure is, "Thelema," meaning *choice, purpose and desire*. The plan of God from the beginning was to have great pleasure in His creation. The very climate of the Garden of Eden resembles pleasure; lush trees, fragrant flowers, exotic birds singing sweetly- and God and His creation enjoying beautiful times together. All that was stripped away in the heat of temptation as Adam and Eve sold out to a deceiving serpent. Bleak! I know, but all is not lost. God labelled His creatures and His creation "redeemed" by the death of His Son Who died on a cruel cross and paid the price for our sin. Realistically, when one looks around today, they would have to ask, "Is God having the pleasure in His creation that He wants?" Well that may be a question that only God can answer, and perhaps the topic for another book. The question that may be easier to answer is, "Is God having pleasure in you and me" Wow! I realize that is a very personal question but it is one that deserves some thought. I have asked myself if God's choice is to have pleasure in us why did He gives us free will, knowing that some would not like Him. I conclude that His choice desire and purpose is to have pleasure in us in spite of us not having pleasure in Him. He has placed Himself in the perimeter to enjoy us, and He does. We are not obligated, programmed nor forced into bringing God pleasure. He enjoys us by virtue of the fact that we are His children. However; we are free to reciprocate.

This presents a dilemma for some of us because we tend to live so far from God and choose to live with a sin and shame mentality that causes us to wonder how God could have pleasure in us. Just for your own interest, some day when you have some time, go to a Christian book store and look at how many books have been written indicating that we are having a wonderful time with God and Him with us. I have not found any material anywhere that covers such a topic. Most of the writings that are "out there" dealing with "God topics" has to do with what He has done, what He is doing and what He is about to do. Materials that support the idea that God is having a good time with His creation are rare. If you have knowledge of such material I would like to know the source so that I may obtain a copy. What I am pointing to is what I have observed over time and that is the connection between us and God appears to be on the head-knowledge level not the intimate or feeling level of bonding with Him.

Would you say that when you experience something that is pleasurable your physical senses are tickled? Does God have sensory pleasure in us? Can we know if God is having pleasure in us? I believe that the answer to all the above is a resounding Yes! The problem is that people who really enjoy God and understand that God finds pleasure in them will tell you that He (God) is so exciting that there are no human words to describe it. Maybe, that is why there is so little written about it.

Part of our "identity" is the pleasure connection with God. It is important to keep in mind that as mentioned previously, God has pleasure in us regardless of ourselves. This is why we were created. But how do we make sense of that? To do so we must understand that, although God enjoys us we are His creation, there is a greater and more significant dimension of pleasure wrapped up in our identity or the image of God that is in us. The story of a woman who poured out all her material wealth is, to me, one of the most heart-warming stories in the Bible; and that touches on this subject significantly.

> *"And being in Bethany in the house of Simon the leper, as He sat at meat, there came a woman having an alabaster box of ointment of spikenard very precious; and she brake the box, and poured it on His head. And there were some that had indignation within themselves, and said, why was this waste of the ointment made? For it might have been sold for more than three hundred pence, and have been given to the poor. And they murmured against her. And Jesus said, Let her alone; why trouble ye her? She hath wrought a good work on me. For ye have the poor with you always, and whensoever ye will ye may do them good: but me ye have not always. She hath done what she could: she is come aforehand to anoint my body to the burying. Verily I say unto you. Wheresoever this gospel shall be preached throughout the whole world, this also that she hath done shall be spoken of for a memorial of her."[25]*

The scene is beyond words. Jesus facing the hour of temptation, the most agonizing journey in His life, and a despised woman is the only one that senses His pain to the point where she brings what some have said was her dowry, all that she had, and poured it on Him. Nice story!! Not! This is the reality of true "connection" with our Maker. He feels the heart beat of every creature and it touches His heart when we "feel Him." This is not just a nice story. It goes to the very core of the preciousness of that which brings pleasure and enjoyment to the Father. This goes beyond feeling God's presence. This is the "pleasure point" that the Father is longing for from all of us; "heart meeting heart." Did you notice that Mary did not say a word to Jesus? Her spirit was in total communion with His. Even the complainers did not distract her. She knew what He needed. This is awesome! So often we go to the Father with our shopping list and we tell Him all our needs and demand that He fix our lives. This is embarrassing to Him as He waits for His children to love on Him. We need to learn the power of silence. Silence penetrates the heart of the Father and melts us into total "oneness" with Him. This is the kind of "oneness" that Jesus talked about in John 17. This "oneness" is not "sameness." It is iden-tification. Without this "ID" we will never really know the joy of enjoying God as He enjoys us. As mentioned before, there is a certain something that transpires between God and His true Worshipers that defies words. When the ointment was running down the body of Jesus, the "ID" card (image) was scanned on both of their hearts and the connection was made. This is one of the reasons that Jesus said that wherever this story, the gospel of connection, is told it would be as a memorial to her. The *"spiritual and emotional data"* would be the same as they both experi-enced. This may be hard to understand, so let's talk a little more about it.

We have talked about "emotional memory" and how it works. It is like a bank account. Most of us have at least one. We put money in them to build up our financial reserves and then we can draw out the money when we need it. Emotional bank account" is used here to explain the dynamics of how we build relationships. In relationships we are constantly building into one another's data base by smiles, kind thoughts, friendliness, providing safety, integrity and so on. This builds trust. Every time we interact we invest in someone and we build up a reserve. The more we interact the more we invest. If we are abusive to someone in anyway, by angry tone in conversation, teasing, name calling or threatening, it puts our "account" in jeopardy. It gets overdrawn. The trust level will drop when it does, we walk on eggs (so to speak) and a sense of mistrust and a feeling of unsafely exist. This can result in divorce, separation, quitting jobs prematurely and children leaving home before they are ready to face the world. When our bank account is empty we make all kinds of foolish decisions. One cannot take from an account that has nothing in it; therefore, we ought to be investing in one another in positive and enjoyable ways all the time. This will ward off such behaviours, as suspicion and fear in our relationships.

The woman who poured out her alabaster box of love on the Lord was in a mind-set of pure worship. Worship is not what we do. Worship is how we are. Put another way worship is how we behave all the time. We can show that we are enjoying God by having Godly behaviour. Let's go over the scene again. A former street woman comes to Jesus and decides to pour all her perfume over Him. The religious people were angry because they were not connected with Him as she was. Many have interpreted this move as sensuous. No! This goes to a higher level, a level that only those who have emptied out their "alabaster box" of pleasure on God will experience and understand.

This is reciprocal pleasure and enjoyment that has absolutely nothing to do with sex or physical attraction. It is pure unadulterated love. Unfortunately, those who do not have an "identification card" like the on-lookers present in the room with Jesus and the woman will interpret it in a carnal manner because they are not connected in this dimension of "oneness." "Oneness" with God was the prayer of Jesus for us and he still desires it today. He desires to enjoy us and we can enjoy Him as we get to know and enjoy ourselves better. The woman was confident in herself as she by-passed the critics and ministered to the Lord.

L = Lovable

Ask most people if they think that they are lovable and the response will be "No." The reason will vary from individual to individual but the main reason will be because of something negative that was done to them or that they did in the past. The beliefs that we have about ourselves are a major factor in whether we fail or succeed in life; whether we just survive or live successfully. Being a lovable person means that we are able to support ourselves on the emotional level.

The information that was given to us in early life does have the power to shape our lives permanently. We can change this but it will take time and effort. The question that needs to be asked is, if we believe that we are unlovable, then how do we make sense of wanting anyone else to love us? This does not make sense. Some of us don't even think about this. We just plug away at life totally oblivious of such details that do affect our lives whether we recognize them or not. Some of us have traded our real self and humanity for our culture to the point that we are truly not at *home*. We are so attuned to what everyone else is doing that we are empty inside. We are not able to take responsibility for our behaviours and actions. We have become somewhat of a loose cannon-out of control and feeling un-lovable. We carry thoughts about our self that are so shameful that we can't tell anyone about them.

Living with repressed thoughts, desires, and feelings are dangerous, and <u>Nathaniel *Branden explains;*</u>

"It is an interesting paradox that repression and emotional self-indulgence are often merely two sides of the same coin. The man who is afraid of his emotions and represses them, sentences himself to be pushed by subconscious motivation–which means, to be ruled by feelings whose existence he dares not identify. And the man who indulges in emotions blindly, has the best reason to be afraid of them—and, at least to some extent, is driven to repress out of self-preservation.

If, then, a man is to avoid repression, he must be prepared to face any thought and any emotion, and to consider them rationally, secure in the conviction that he will not act without knowing what he is doing and why.

Ignorance is not bliss, not in any area of man's life, and certainly not with regard to the contents of his own mind"[26]

When we were children we had little or no control over many of the things that transpired in our lives. It is obvious that some of us were abused, leaving us with emotional scars and wounds... As we mature physically we learn to take our lives in control and eliminate the negative images that can hinder us. If we choose to keep those images they will become our "leaders and controllers." We must keep in mind that we are not responsible for other people's behaviours, just our own. If the negative behaviours of people in the past have overshadowed our lives we need to deal with them; otherwise they will continue to control us. If we choose to work through them and move on, it will have to be done methodically. First, individuals must decide that they deserve to be happy and enjoy their life. They must also decide to forgive those that hurt them and then they can start to work out the pain that is deep inside. A big mistake that some people make is to believe that they can pray away deep inner pain; it doesn't work. Inner pain calls for "inner work." We can allow Holy Spirit to work and set us free from the past, helping us to see that we are lovable and enjoyable.

F = Fulfilled

I think that almost everyone would like to experience a fulfilled life; one that is exciting and celebrative. The world has its own interpretation of fulfillment. We see people struggling to find *the American dream*. In many ways this dream has become a nightmare. For some this is because the process of getting the dream fulfilled has caused many to lose their way as human beings. We end up in a "dog eat dog" world were cheating, deception and criminal activities abound. Some have lost the ability to be honest and fair in every-day business dealings. Lies and cheating are seen as "normal" business practices.

There was a time when a hand-shake could settle a business deal. People were able to trust one another. Today, we must get Lawyers involved to sort through the smallest transaction due to crookedness and deception. This is truly a sign of the times we live in. Even families members are taking each other to court to fight for money and other things. This is another sign of the dangerous times that we are in. Sex is getting more marketable and is a huge part of the world's "commodity." God intended sex to be a strong and Godly part of our whole and sacred image. — Perhaps this is a topic for another book.

What sort of legacy are we leaving for our children? They need families, friends and a community that are morally and ethically sound. It is wonderful to support our children materially, but we need to show them Christ-like examples and guide them in making good choices for their lives. It has become a challenge for many parents to raise their children in a society where so much corruption exists, but we must take heart because there is hope. We can still choose to instil good values in our children and in our selves. How do we do this in a society that has values that are based on the material world rather than the eternal world? This is not easy to change but it is totally possible. The following, are some of the power-tools for alleviating the ***crisis: identity.***

Finding Our Identity Card

We must make a decision to find our ***identity card***. It holds the information for living a fulfilled life. We can also make a decision to seek for God until we find Him. He has invited us to do so. We can find the real fullness of life in His Son Jesus Christ. In Him we are fulfilled.

> *"And ye shall seek me, and find me, when ye shall search for me with all your heart"* [27]

We must also choose the godly standards given by Jesus to not judge others.

> *"Judge not, that ye be not judged."* [28]

We need to decide to lay aside all the blame, shame and guilt from self and others.

> *"….that we should be holy and without blame before him in love:"* [29]

When we are emptied of all inner pain we will feel fulfilled. Enjoying God as our Father will become a natural thing and it will cause us to reverence Him as our King and enjoy Him as our Father. This was His plan from the beginning. It is not possible to know God and enjoy Him when there is a big "mess" inside our hearts.

Do not disrespect anyone. Showing respect for God's creation is respecting God. Treating everyone in the same respectful manner is God's will.

"My brethren, have not the faith of our Lord Jesus Christ, the Lord of glory, with respect of persons. For there come unto your assembly a man with a gold ring, in goodly apparel, and there came in also a poor man in vile raiment; And ye have respect to him that weareth the gay clothing, and say unto him, Sit thou here in a good place; and say to the poor, Stand thou there, or sit thou here under my footstool: Are ye not then partial in yourselves, and are become judges of evil thoughts?"[30]

Because our feelings and behaviours are governed by our thoughts we must streamline them to be clean and pure.

"Finally, brethren, whatsoever things are true, whatsoever things are honest, whatsoever things are just, whatsoever things are pure, whatsoever things are lovely, whatsoever things are of good report; if there be any virtue, and if there be any praise, think on these things"[31]

We are admonished by the Apostle Paul to say prayers for all people. This carries the potential to bring people together.

"I exhort therefore, that, first of all, supplications, prayers, intercession, and giving of thanks, be made for all men; For kings, and for all that are in authority; that we may lead a quiet and peaceful life in all godliness and honesty. For this is good and acceptable in the sight of God our Saviour;"[32]

Know God's plan for your life. This will prevent you from listening to ideas that will set you back. This is what God said.

> *"For I know the thoughts that I think toward you, saith the Lord, thoughts of peace, and not of evil, to give you an expected end."*[33]

Involvement in our community plays a part in shaping our lives.

> *"Having your conversation honest among the Gentiles: that, whereas they speak against you as evildoers, they may by your good works, which they shall behold, glorify God in the day of visitation"*[34]

Care and concern must be shown to all people and indeed to our families.

> *"As we have therefore opportunity, let us do good unto all men, especially to them who are of the household of faith."*[35]

The creation of God reveals His majesty and they are all around us to be appreciated and enjoy. Take time to enjoy the beauty of nature.

> *"The heavens declare the glory of God; and the firmament sheweth his handy work"*[36]

The love of God forms a banner of love all around us. We need to accept it and call it our own:

"He brought me to his banqueting house, and his banner over me was love."[37]

We must be committed to on-going emotional investment in God ourselves and others.

"Wherefore comfort yourselves together, and edify one another, even as also ye do"[38]

The words of God are so precious and life giving. We must constantly put them in our hearts"

"To know wisdom and instruction; to perceive the words of understanding; To receive the instruction of wisdom, justice, and judgment, and equity;"[39]

There will be times when we face challenges that will cause us to have questions but, with the strength of the Lord, we can stay strong in God's word and receive the help that we need.

"And straightway the father of the child cried out, and said with tears, Lord, I believe; help thou mine unbelief."[40]

This reflects the identification strategy and the acronym spells identification (see Model 6). Once again let me remind you that you are loved and, if you haven't already done this, tell yourself that. As God's beautiful creation, you deserve love. Now, let that fragrance of God's love ascend from your heart to the One who made you for His pleasure and ban the ***crisis: identity.***

Model # 6

Here is your ID card!
Identification card.

Invest in yourself by inviting Jesus Christ into your life.
Decide to stop criticizing yourself and everyone else.
Empty yourself of any blame, shame, guilt and enjoy God and yourself.
Never disrespect anyone.
Think positively and purely.
Include all people in your prayers.
Familiarize yourself with the truth that God said about you.
Involve yourself in your community.
Care for all people, especially your family.
Appreciate all the beauty that God made.
Tell yourself daily that you are loved.
Invest positively in the emotional bank of everyone including yourself.
Open your heart to learning God's Word.
Never doubt God or yourself.

Chapter # 4

Come Home,
It's Safe Now

Now that you have received your "ID card," do you want to come home?

It is safe to return _home_ if you have done that which is necessary to make your _home_ safe and reinforced. As mentioned previously there are four building blocks that are also necessary to have in place in order to feel safe at _home._ They are: Acceptance, Affection, Appreciation and Attention. These building blocks are to be set in place in childhood by our care-givers. If that did not take place do not despair. It is not too late! Adults are able to set them up for themselves. Here is the first one.

Acceptance

Definition of acceptance; unconditional affirmation of ourselves, regardless of how we appear. It is only as we accept ourselves on this level that we can appropriately change the things that need to be changed.

Self-acceptance is the key to accepting God and others. Without it we struggle to really love others as Jesus asked us to do. As mentioned before, He has commanded us to love one another as He loves. In Romans 5:8 we read that the love of God has been put in our hearts. This being true, it would appear that we have the ability to love. Two problems exist, however; one; the heart must be clean for this love to show through, and two; self-care (often confused with pride) must be a regular activity. Some people say that if they put any emphasis on self whatsoever, God won't be pleased with them. The truth of the matter is, if there is no Godly self-care how can we truly please God? When pride and self-love becomes mixed up, we have confusion. Self-care is different from pride and self-indulgence. Self-care is a pre-requisite to self-love and acceptance because the Lord inhabits our bodies as His temple. On the other hand pride is a demonstration of self exaltation which God hates. Humility is total dependence on God. Through this dependence we can accept and love ourselves the way that we should.

Affection

Definition for affection; An embrace of the heart to self and others.[dmc] We all need healthy affection which is a sense of comfort in the heart, and a feeling of belonging. This goes beyond physical touching. It is like being cuddled by loving gentle hands and having a sense of permanent inner security and comfort. Lack of healthy affection puts us in a world of isolation, loneliness and lack of self expression. The lack of it could be one of the reasons we left *home* in the first place. Leaving *home* causes us to fill the emptiness inside with all kinds of wrong substitutes (e.g. cigarettes, alcohol, drugs, food, inappropriate relationships and behaviours). When there is a sense of real comfort in the heart, life takes on new meaning and we feel connected. Care-givers are strategically given by God to show and express healthy affection. Without this experience of enmeshment with care-givers, children will not develop the ability to show love and receive healthy love. They will live in a state of emptiness and abandonment which also creates the framework for misuse of their sexuality.

Children have a need to feel parental affection and to be welcomed in the world. So often we hear stories of children being neglected and left to feel unappreciated and unloved. These children will become like empty houses without proper foundations. Acceptance, affection, approval and attention cause children to be centered, grounded, self-accepting and confident. They begin life with a greater understanding of their personal value-systems rather than vices. Values include responsibility, honesty, dignity and integrity. Being appreciated early in life is a marvellous tool against co-dependency and fosters interdependency. They are great tools to help structure healthy boundaries.

Approval

Definition; the largest OK sign in the world and it is written on every heart by God

Have you ever looked for a product on the shelf and found yourself looking for a certain seal or name? Likely this will be one that you have used previously with good result. You desire the product again because it has been given your seal of approval. This is very interesting. We use a product which carries a good reputation and brings satisfaction, so we go to find that same product again. How is it that we can do this to an inanimate object but we sometimes find it difficult to give ourselves approval?

Is it not because our original negative data system, loaded with disapproval, handed down to us in our early years still prevails? Some call it the "negative tapes." I will call it the "phantom reel." The "phantom reel" is the inner movie that is being watched and felt constantly in the subconscious mind. The subconscious mind is working all the time, even when we sleep. It takes in information from our environment and, as strange as it may sound, this was happening from before we were conceived. I believe that we came in the world with information that was in our mother and it was transferred to us in the womb through *feeling tones*. Our subconscious is embedded in feeling tones. Feelings began in the womb. Information that is pleasant, positive and uplifting causes the subconscious mind to produce good feelings and negative information causes negative feelings. Positive and negative information from the environment goes to the subconscious mind for investigation and storage. Because we were created in God's image and likeness the mind can only make sense of information that brings encouragement and edification and causes positive *feeling tones.* Negative information causes discouragement and is the main root of anger. If this is left un-attended for a long time it will cause numerous problems. This is one of the reasons so many people revert to anger when they feel stuck. Too many negatives have been festering inside them. The subconscious mind will spend little time on storing positive information in a special part of the brain which is like a reservoir for self preservation. This information will stay in short or long term memory and is drawn upon later for gratification. However, if the information is negative the mind attaches a code or a dirge tone to the information. This is much like a filing system where certain items are flagged. It files the information in *feeling tones.* Negative information about self has a very low tone which is the feeling a person gets when they are depressed and is much like a dirge. Positive information carries a high tone much like a beautiful well blended choir. Anger is felt when something is heard or an action is seen. The subconscious picks up the ***dirge tone file*** and that is connected to what is going on in the present environment. Anger being the most negative, self-preserving and damaging emotion surfaces because it is the emotion that carries the power to get attention and, even though, for the most part, it is negative attention, it will bring a temporary gratification or restoration of personal power. Positive occurrences tend to generate laughter and other positive emotions, because that is the data- connection that was stored in our **tone bank.** Child-hood disapproval and rejection caused us to abandon self. This information also goes in our **tone bank** filing system. Approval from care-givers in early life creates meaning, self-value and purpose. Once this happens life becomes worthwhile. Our main purpose is to bring pleasure and glory to God and this is already coded in the image of God in our ***human bar-code***. However, if something took place in our lives that marred this image, we need to give ourselves the permission to mentally put the sign of approval right across our chest. Self-approval is a very massive topic and cannot be treated in its entirety here. However, until we are able to feel self-approved we will very easy fall into all kinds of addictions. Self-approval prevents addictions.

Definition for addiction: Leaning on air. [Dmc]

Attention

So often we see children behaving in negative ways and their behaviour is sometimes interpreted by some people as *attention seeking*. When a child feels neglected and out of place they tend to behave in ways that will get attention from adults to help them feel connected. If the child receives a negative reaction to his behaviour due to the frustration of the care-giver, the child learns the negative emotional transfer from the care-giver and disregards the lesson that was intended. This reaction can be as simple as a raised voice or a negative stare. The reason for this is every verbal or physical expression carries data. This data is what the child reads and stores in her _**tone bank**_. The child is seeking positive emotions to put in her bank. She is basically seeking "emotional investments" that will help to develop her female[41] identity. For example, children are like empty canvases on which we place musical notes for them to sing later on in their lives. If you have difficulty believing this, next time something happens in your life check to see which "emotional note" comes up. This is a major topic one for another book. The closer the child feels to the care-giver, the more they will realize the image of God and have a greater "sense of self." The adult must give the child the "OK" to see himself as God's image. This is called validation. Positive attention in a child's life provides him with the tools to deal with difficulties such as bullying, teasing and boundary setting because his "self-image" ultimately is realized in God's image. Validation decreases attention seeking.

It is rather difficult to present children with validated "identification cards" until the parents possess them.

Becoming Response-able

Can you recall being given a task you felt you were not equipped to do? Can you recall the feelings that ensued? Were they nervousness and fear? Many times we are called upon to do something that we are not trained to do but, for whatever reason, we try to do it. Sometimes we succeed at it and sometimes we fail. There are other times when, even though we are not trained to do something, trial and error brings us major success because we persevered. God did not intend for us to live by trial and error. His plan for us is to be totally equipped to face life so we can be successful in whatever we do and, more importantly, in how we see ourselves. The success that we want to focus on here is success in becoming a ***human being.*** This means we know who we are and we are thankful to God for who we are and not just for what we achieve and possess materially. The other side of the coin is, when adults are not living as God intended, they ***become human doings;*** which means they are approval seekers. As a result, far too much emphasis is placed on what we ***do*** instead of the person we are. In most circles of western society, after meeting someone for the first time, one of the first questions that will be asked is, "What is your name?" It is very likely the next question will be, "What do you do?" It appears that our professions or careers make us who we are. This question then appears to be loaded because many times they determine how we are treated by some people. Let's face it, we can't do much about that; at least not until we understand how important it is to ***be*** who God intended us to ***be.***

The question that must be asked is, "How do we become ***response-able*** to the place where we are aware of who we are and take responsibility for all our behaviours?"

Most people have become ***reactors.*** They react to most things in life. They become emotionally involved at the drop of a hat. They do not take the time to get details before they set their judgments, criticisms, ridicule and analysis are in place. This kind of behaviour is dangerous, damaging and devilish but it happens all the time. <u>R</u>*eactors* are everywhere. They are in the pulpits of the world, the parliaments, homes and places of business. They are like a time-bomb ready to explode at any time. They cause an environment of emergency and volatility. On the other hand there are the ***responders.*** These are the people that *"have it all together."* They have learned how not to use negative emotions to deal with people and situations. If we desire to be responders investment in self-awareness will be beneficial toward dealing with problems appropriately. Some people will say that it is not possible to behave as the latter and be *normal*. It is! We will find out what makes ***reactors*** and what makes ***responders***. Both behaviours are learned and chosen. If one had a negative up-bringing it will be more challenging to learn to be a ***responder***; but it is possible. The more abuse we experience in our early years the further we go from being able to respond to life's challenges; and we will find it much easier to react. This is due to the unmanageability of the pain which caused us to leave ourselves which is our ***home.*** This is in a sense like when there is a fire in our house and we run outside.

Child-hood abuse took me from ***home*** to a place where I was scared and lonely. Leaving ***home*** meant that I was too scared to be with myself. I lost my ***Identification card***, but the Lord returned it through a connection with Himself. His image had to be restored in me. Leaving ***home*** filled my heart with anger. I would get angry when things did not go the way that I wanted them. This was a common thing and I can still hear myself saying at each blow-up, "I can't help it. I am sorry." That was my belief. Back then I truly believed that I was not able to do much about my anger beside manage it the best I could. I learned later on that one does not manage anger. Instead they find the cause of their anger and deal with that. By taking time to allow Holy Spirit to work out for me the reasons for the anger, I have learned to manage myself and my behaviours instead of trying to manage the anger. Trying to manage anger is a waste of time. I can still be angry if I choose to, but I have learned not to use a negative emotion such as anger to deal with life's problems, not to mention, dealing with people. Anger has a way of clouding reason and I think it is better to reason than react. Even God, when dealing with sin issues in the Old Testament, called the people to reason. The Prophet Isaiah writes;

"Come now, and let us reason together, saith the Lord: Though your sin be as scarlet, they shall be as white as snow; though they be red like crimson, they shall be as wool."[42]

Some people believe that God does whatever He wants to do both in their lives and in the world. From what I have learned and experienced, this is not true. I believe that God does what He says. The Bible confirms this. In the case of Sodom and Gomorrah the Lord was very clear on what He was about to do. I believe that doing this gives us a chance to reason and repent.

"And the Lord said, Shall I hide from Abraham that thing which I do; ...And the Lord said because

the cry of Sodom and Gomorrah is great, and because their sin is very grievous; I will go down now, and see whether they have done altogether according to the cry of it, which is come unto me; and if not I will know. ...And Abraham drew near, and said, Wilt thou also destroy the righteous with the wicked? Peradventure there be fifty righteous in the city: wilt thou also destroy and not spare the place for the fifty righteous that are therein? That be far from thee to do after this manner, to slay the righteous with the wicked: and that the righteous should be as the wicked, that be far from thee: Shall not the Judge of all the earth do right? And the Lord said, if I find in Sodom fifty righteous within the city, then I will spare all the place for their sakes. And Abraham answered and said, Behold now, I have taken upon me to speak unto the Lord, which am but dust and ashes: Peradventure there should lack five of the fifty righteous: wilt thou destroy all the city for lack of five? And he said, If I find there forty and five, I will not destroy it. ... And he said, Oh let not the Lord be angry, and I will speak yet but this once: Peradventure ten shall be found there. And he said. I will not destroy it for ten's sake. And the Lord went his way, as soon as he had left communing with Abraham: and Abraham returned to his place."[43]

It shows that God doesn't act on a whim; He is reasonable as shown here with Abraham. The ability to be **_response-able_** is a part of the **_human bar code_**; regardless of negative things that have happened in our lives that indicates otherwise. Because the image of God is in us we already have a head-start on being ***response-able*** and this will lead to behaviour that is designed for God's glory.

Model # 7

Behaviour by Design

Behaviour by design is a breath of fresh air to me. It highlights key reasons why we behave in certain ways and supports those who desire to structure their behaviours. I have seen programs designed specifically to help people with acquired brain injury that have been very effective in helping them to work through behavioural difficulties. There are certain brain functions that change after someone experiences a brain injury. In many cases, depending on the extent of the injury, normal functions tend to return very slowly. I have also personally witnessed these improvements as I worked with those who experienced brain injury and I have thought that, if programs designed for improving and enhancing positive behaviour can have such outstanding results, why is it that people who claim to know God behave negatively and irresponsibly when the Word of God guides us toward ***excellent behaviours?***

Behaviour by design is a comprehensive tool formulated to put good behaviour in perspective. However, our value system must be clearly defined. Values such as integrity, sincerity, nobility and honesty are fundamental to those who desire to behave well. This is made possible by having an understanding of their God-image and their self-image. Self-image plays a very big part in behaving well and seeing ourselves as capable of achieving anything worthwhile in life. Joe Alexander writes;

> *"It is important to have a positive mental image of yourself that is based on reality and not on illusion. In other words, when it comes to a positive self-image, don't kid yourself. If you are a functioning person and getting by, then you are capable of being honest with yourself. You know what you can do based on your experience. What you don't know is that most likely there are many things you can do you have never tried because of some negativity in your self-image."[44]*

God's image (potential) is rooted in the human spirit. Having a good self-image is wonderful but any image that we have that is not rooted in God's image is a false image and carries the potential of idolatry.

Behaviour by design is a process that can be very successful but vigilance is needed, because many things will try to prevent the process. Among them are *hijackers.* I call them *hijackers* because of their ability to stop the healthy process of good behaviour in mid stream. The diagram below shows how *hijackers* work. They are internal and external forces that come to relinquishing our God-given right to be leaders of ourselves and take *response-ability* for our actions, not blaming anyone. Holy Spirit is on hand to help if we call.

Behaviour by Design

1	2	3	4	5
You made me do it	You make me feel bad	You make me think	You make me angry	You frustrate me all the time
Relinquish Response-ability	Easy way out	No self-control	Emotional Behaviour transfer	Blame mechanism

The top row is <u>hijacker</u> statements. The result of this understanding is shown in the bottom row.

The first step to take in designing your behaviour is to ask yourself, "Who is in control of your life?" If the answer to that question is God and yourself, *<u>behaviour by design</u>* is for you. The next step is, once you make the decision to change your behaviour, you will need to use these strategies every day until the new behaviours become a part of your life.

Strategies for Behaviour by Design

1. Remember you have the ability to make choices.
2. No one is in control of your emotions except you.
3. You can think for yourself.
4. No one can make you angry. Only you can choose to be angry.

5. Choose positive emotions to deal with challenges. Avoid frustration and anger.

Model # 8

The next strategy for behaving well is called, M-R-I, properly called, ***my response indicator***. It is designed to help whenever a challenging situation appears and to give support in designing a good behaviour.

This strategy we will call an MRI

"My Response Indicator"

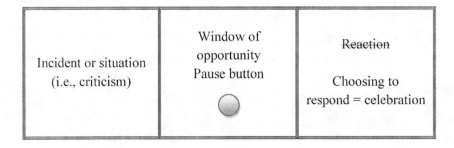

Incident or situation (i.e., criticism)	Window of opportunity Pause button	~~Reaction~~ Choosing to respond = celebration

The first window shows an incident has taken place. Let's say someone criticized you. The second window shows a button which indicates a pause. This button can be pushed mentally to give yourself time to decide how you want to response instead of reacting. This is your ***power indicator button*** showing that ***you*** are in control, not the situation, and definitely not other people. It is also called your **_window of opportunity_** to take a good look at the fact that no one else can **_make you go out of control_**.... Nothing pleases our heavenly Father more than good behaving children and it is possible for us to behave well for God's glory. Negative behaviour is an indication of not being at **_home._** The road to having world peace through Godly behaviour may take a while and abuses in child-hood could be the biggest giant to overcome. The strategies given here are only a few of the support systems available to us. There are others; but for now, here is the final one.

Model # 9

Wait......Relate......Contemplate......Formulate

Whenever you are faced with a situation that seems bigger than yourself, remember to Wait......Relate...... Contemplate......and Formulate before you decide on what action to take. This means to process your actions, agree with yourself (head and heart), then implement the plan. This plan will always keep you from using negative emotions to deal with people and life's challenging situations. You can decide the proper action to take in order to eliminate more crises. Using negative emotions to deal with people can scar them for life. This place of inner stabilization is being at **_home_** in the image of God. It is about self-respect and honouring the image of God and acting like God. This is the blue-print for a celebrative life. This will help us to know ourselves more. Knowing who we are will cause us to love our neighbours and we will not hurt them. We will protect them. While "world peace" may not be seen around the corner, believe me, it is there. World peace starts inside each one of us and spreads to each person in our homes with love, care, respect, honour, gratitude etc; then slowly like a beautiful flowing stream it spreads out and bursts into the sea of our community and across the world. The ability to ***heal*** this broken world is in our hands and we can take our ID card, which ultimately is the God-image in us, and start to repair the damage that we have done to ourselves and one another. If we all begin to take our ***Identification Cards*** and use them, we will STOP ***CRISIS: IDENTITY.***

End Notes

1 John 14: 15 - 20
2 Galatians 4:4-6
3 "Experiencing Father's Embrace" Pg 2-3 P 4-6
4"Experiencing Father's Embrace" P# 7 P # 3

5 Psalms 23: 1-6
6 Mark 2:4-5
7 1 Kings, 30:6
8 John 16: 7, 13
9 "Safe People" Pg # 151, p.5
10 Matthew 13: 30
11 Charles R Swindoll "Living Beyond the Daily Grind" pg# 142 p3 "
12 See John 13:35
13 John Bradshaw: "Creating Love" Pg #265- P3, 266 P # 1
14 Hebrews 2: 5-8
15 Psalms 139: 13-16

16 "Total Life Management" Pg # 86 P 1-2
17 "Don't Sweat the Small Stuff" Pg # 112 P #2
18 "Telling yourself the truth" PG #52 P1
19 "The art of understanding yourself" Pg #161 P.1
20 "The art of understanding yourself" Pg 168 P# 5,169 P1-5
21 Psalms 145 8-9
22 "The Pummeled Heart" Pg# 60 P 3-4
23 John 17: 21
24 Revelation 4:11

25 Mark 14:3-9
26 "The psychology of self-esteem" Pg # 87-88 4-5
27 Jeremiah 29:13
28 Matthew 7:1
29 Ephesians 1:4
30 James2:1-4
31 Phillipians4:8
32 1 Timothy 2: 1-3
33 Jeremiah 29: 11
34 1 Peter 2:12
35 Galatians 6:10
36 Psalms 19:1
37 Song of Solomon 2:4
38 1 Thessalonians 5:11
39 Proverbs 1:2-3
40 Mark 9:24

41 Anywhere female gender is used it can be changed to male and vice versa.
42 Isaiah 1: 18
43 Genesis 18: 17, 20, 21, 23-28, 32-33
44 "Dare to Change" Pg # 56-57

Bibliography

All Bible References from <u>Dakes Annotated Reference Bible</u>
Dakes Bible Sales Inc Po Box 625 Lawrenceville, Georgia 30246 © 1963

<u>Experiencing Father's Embrace</u>
by Jack Frost
Published by Father's House Productions Inc.
P.O. Box 37
Conway, SC 20528
843-369-2004

<u>Safe People</u> by Dr. Henry Cloud and
Dr. John Townsend
By Dr. Henry Cloud and Dr. John Townsend
Zondervan Publishing House
Grand Rapids, Michigan 49530

<u>Living Beyond The Daily Grind: Reflections On the Songs and Sayings of Scripture (Book 1)</u> by Charles R. Swindoll.
Copyright 1988 by Charles R Swindoll

Creating Love by John Bradshaw
By John Bradshaw
Bantam Books, New York,
New York 10036

Total Life Management by Robert R. Shank
© 1990 by Robert R. Shank
Published by Multnomah Press
Portland, Oregon 97266

Don't Sweat The Small Stuff
by Richard Carlson, Ph. D.
Copyright © 1998 by Richard Carlson, Ph. D.
114 Fifth Ave, New York,
New York 10011

Telling yourself the Truth By Marie Chapian and William
Backus
Copyright © 1980 by Marie Chapian and William Backus
Published by Bethany House Publishers
11300 Hampshire Avenue South
Minneapolis, Minnesota 55438

The Art of Understanding Yourself
by Cecil G. Osborne
Copyright © 1967 by Zondervan Publishing House
1415 Lake Drive, S.E.,
Grand Rapids. Michigan 49506

The Pummeled Heart by Antoinette Bosco
© Copyright 1994 Antoinette Bosco
By Twenty Third Publications
P.O. Box 180
Mystic, CT 06355

The Psychology of Self-Esteem
by Nathaniel Branden
Copyright © 1969 by Nathaniel Branden
C/o Gerard McCauley Agency, Inc.,
141 E. 44 St., New York,
N Y 10017

Dare To Change by Joe Alexander
Copyright © 1986 by Joe Alexander
NAL PENGUIN INC.,
1633 Broadway, New York,
New York 10019

Printed in the United States
121223LV00001B/54/P

9 781606 470947